"Ambitious. . . . [A] sharp, engagingly composed study of the multiple kinds of fragmentation that torment the American self in the post-everything information age. . . . Conley brings an astutely conditioned—and suitably jaundiced—eye to the task of tracking the permanently distracted self through its new placeless habitat." —Tom Vanderbilt, *BookForum*

"Conley is a debunker. . . . [He] connects the dots in new ways and brings in research that may contradict what readers think they know." —*Forbes*

"Usefully summarizes all sorts of far-flung academic research while repurposing the latest pop-sociological idea entrepreneurship, from Chris Anderson's 'long tail' to Richard Florida's 'creative class.'" —*The New York Times Book Review*

"This brilliant new book makes sense of how changes in the ways people work are affecting the ways families work. Conley writes with the grace of a novelist and the insight of a rigorous scholar." —Richard Sennett, author of *The Craftsman*

"Convincing. . . . Intelligent. . . . This book was written before the dawning of the neo-Depression now deepening around us, and many of its insights feel more ominous now." —*The Seattle Times*

"Compelling. . . . A measured mix of social science, first-person reporting and historical research." —*Newsday*

"Put down your iPhones and BlackBerrys, dear friends, long enough to read this important book about America's new 'elsewhere society,' where round-the-clock connectivity and multitasking are reshaping the most basic patterns of work, family, and values. Your guide to this brave new world is Dalton Conley, one of America's most brilliant and perspective social commentators and scholars, and an excellent and entertaining writer as well. No other book compares in describing and explaining the texture of modern lives in a hypernetworked and hypermarketized world. Conley's insights might just help to rescue the 'priceless' from the credit card ads and restore it to work, family, friends, and identity, all of which are under siege in our elsewhere society." —Jeffrey D. Sachs, author of *The End of Poverty*

"A sobering and fearlessly honest account of our lives, of your life. . . . A must-read." —*Sacramento Book Review*

"Conley is spot-on in his analysis of our hyperconnected world. In these days of BlackBerry ubiquity, it's useful to have an experienced guide to help make sense of it all—and maybe convince us to unplug once in a while." —*St. Petersburg Times*

"Scintillating. . . . Always compelling. . . . Conjures useful talking points on some of the most salient social dynamics of our time." —*The Wichita Eagle*

"Brilliant and, at times, chilling. . . . A sociological mirror, this book is equal parts cautionary tale, exercise in contemporary anthropology and a spiritual and emotional audit of the twenty-first-century American." —*Publishers Weekly*

"No one has written about how we live today more vividly, and more accurately, than Dalton Conley. *Elsewhere, U.S.A.* explains the multitude of changes—technological, economic, psychological, cultural—that have affected us in recent years, and he makes it possible to find out who we are now as Americans, and why." —Richard Florida, author of *The Rise of the Creative Class*

DALTON CONLEY

Elsewhere, U.S.A.

Dalton Conley is University Professor and Dean for the Social Sciences at New York University. He also teaches at NYU's Wagner School of Public Service, as an Adjunct Professor of Community Medicine at Mount Sinai School of Medicine, and he is a Research Associate at the National Bureau of Economic Research. His essays have appeared in *The New York Times*, the *Los Angeles Times*, *Forbes*, and *Slate*, among other publications. His previous books include *Honky*; *Being Black, Living in the Red: Race, Wealth, and Social Policy in America*; and *The Pecking Order: Which Siblings Succeed and Why*. Conley lives in New York City.

ALSO BY DALTON CONLEY

The Pecking Order

You May Ask Yourself

After the Bell

The Starting Gate

Wealth and Poverty in America

Honky

Being Black, Living in the Red

Social Class

Elsewhere, U.S.A.

Elsewhere, U.S.A.

DALTON CONLEY

Vintage Books
A Division of Random House, Inc.
New York

The Library of Congress has cataloged the Pantheon edition as follows:
Conley, Dalton.
Elsewhere, U.S.A. / Dalton Conley.
p. cm.
1. Social change.   2. Social structure.   3. Social problems.
4. Economic indicators.   5. Social indicators.   I. Title.
HM831.C654 2008
306.0973'09045—dc22
2007050081

Vintage ISBN: 978-1-4000-7679-6

Author photograph © Lisa Ackerman
Book design by M. Kristen Bearse

www.vintagebooks.com

Printed in the United States of America
10 9 8 7 6 5 4 3 2 1

TO NATALIE,

MY PARTNER HERE, THERE, AND ELSEWHERE

Contents

Preface

My maternal grandparents were married for more than fifty years. He was the town dentist of Carbondale, Pennsylvania, and she was his homemaker partner. As a professional couple in a mostly working-class, coal-mining community, they enjoyed a rich social life. They played bridge on the weekends, going so far as to compete in the statewide circuit of tournaments. They also played golf a couple times a week—sharing a drink with their professional friends afterward as they swapped jokes about Jesus and Moses playing the water hole. With some occasional substitutions, they always seemed to tee up with the same couples: another dentist and his wife, a doctor and his wife, and the owner of the local Ford dealership and his wife. None of these college-educated women worked, though many of them appeared (to me at least) to be a notch or two brighter than their husbands.

As my grandmother put it: Grandpa is in charge of the outside, and I am in charge of the inside. She meant that he took care of mowing the lawn and weeding their vegetable garden, while she was responsible for keeping house and entertaining. But I never thought such an arrangement was quite fair, since I saw the inside to be the 1,200-square-foot house and the outside to stretch to the ends of the known universe. But the system seemed—from outward appearances—to work. Roles and authority were never questioned. And no one ever raised a voice in their home; in fact, still today, if I need to conjure up a calming, peaceful image, I think of sitting in a rocking chair on their porch, talking about my summer plans.

Of course, I remember their lives through the idealized glasses of a child. But there are some basic facts that cannot be disputed. For example, though my grandfather enjoyed his work, he saved and invested his money as best he could so that he could retire early. And retire early he did—by his mid-fifties the only teeth he pulled were those of my sister and me when we went for our annual checkup in his Depression-era basement chair. Work was simply something you did and hopefully enjoyed, but it was something you strove to leave behind as soon as you were financially able to lead "the good life." For them, the good life entailed paid off mortgages, kids through college, and a condo in Florida where they could spend the winter months and play golf more than twice a week. Perhaps, then, it is fitting (or even ironic) that my grandfather, who lived to a ripe age of eighty-one, died thanks to his favorite leisure activity. While playing golf in Florida in 1989, his friend lost control of the motorized golf cart and ran him over. A few days later, he died of heart failure.

Perhaps the absurdity of the accident sparked my grandmother's irrepressible humor. But for the fifteen years afterward that she lived on, she would remark that perhaps it was best that he died the way he did. "He always said he wanted to die on a golf course after hitting a hole in one," she would say, perhaps unaware of the renowned scene from the film *Caddyshack*, which depicted just that. "He'll have to settle for par." The real reason it was all for the best, she'd add in a more serious tone, was that his health was beginning to fail him anyway—and it's better, she'd argue, to go quickly than to wither away.

My own parents' marriage represented quite a different

arrangement to that of my mother's folks. My father did the cooking. Both pursued careers that were ends in and of themselves. Earning money was secondary in the 1960s and '70s. He, an artist, has painted acrylics on canvas long before and long after his day job ended. He soldiers on, forsaking the New York art world, to which he had moved from Connecticut via Wisconsin. Today, he paints daily in a large garage-based studio in rural Pennsylvania, not far from where my mother was raised. She, meanwhile, continues to write books long after her flash of success in the early 1980s has been forgotten and publishers have moved on to the latest hot, young author.

They never learned to play golf or bridge. For them, leisure meant throwing or attending a dinner party with their group of bohemian friends. Or perhaps going to an art opening. Or maybe, if my mother could convince my father, going to a literary reading. But as they got older, mostly their free time meant watching television or reading, for my mother, and exercising or watching sports, for my father. They, of course, don't have as much free time as my grandparents since they still work at their chosen vocation every day.

As children both my parents were given bikes and free-range of the small towns in which they lived, whereas my sister and I had to learn to navigate the dangerous world of New York City in the 1970s. That meant a lot shorter radius of freedom. It also meant learning the bus, and later, the subway system. And it meant that socializing for us had to be prearranged, often involving sleepovers. In fact, the first time my sister was allowed to go outside and roam the city without an adult was January 22, 1984. She was eleven. This date was forever etched into our consciousness since it was preserved for posterity by the *New York Times,* in a story the paper ran on the revitalization of lower Broadway. At first my mother thought it must have been a pervert who was bothering her daughter and her friends when Alexandra recounted the story. But the next day, the proof was there in black and white: "Down the block at Tower Records, the midday rush was reaching a crescendo," wrote John Duka in the Metro Section.

"Lower Broadway is New Wave," said Alexandra Conley, 11 years old, as she and a group of her friends who live in the neighborhood headed for the back of the store.

"It's in," piped Johanna Jackson, 11.

"What's really good about this neighborhood," said Jessica Nudel, 11, as she cleared her throat to silence the shuffling of a group of boys who joined them, "what's really good, is that it used to be all burned out, you know, but now you can be a kid and walk anywhere without being afraid."

"Gosh, is she smart," said a boy in a blue parka. At that, Jessica, Johanna and Alexandra all rolled their eyes, jumped up and down like hot popcorn and fell upon the nearest stack of 45's.

Today, though New York City is way safer than it was in 1984, I could not imagine letting my ten-year-old daughter walk the four blocks to school by herself, let alone hang out in Tower Records (now defunct, the building snapped up by my employer, New York University—but that's a different, if related story about the transformation of the urban economy). She would hardly have time, anyway. As I write this, she is busy with ice-skating lessons. Yesterday was piano, and the day before was French. This is all piled on top of homework, online math tutorials, and other after-school activities. Not to mention being dragged along to academic lectures, on business trips, and to playdates where the parents want to get to know one another, so they thrust unfamiliar kids (roughly the same age) into a room together as the grown-ups sip coffee. And besides, my children's own friends are much more in flux. Whereas Alexandra is *still* best friends with the very same Johanna mentioned in the 1984 article, my daughter's best friend just moved to Tokyo with her mother, who landed a huge promotion there (leaving her brother and father behind in New York—and, no, they are not getting divorced). It may be a crazy arrangement, but it is by no means unique. My own sister's husband just got relocated to Italy for nine months—not enough time for her to learn the language and start up a new career with two young children, so she is staying in the United States. And my wife's boss and his spouse split their time between New York, where he works, and Israel, where she does.

Leisure? The "good life"? What are those? Work is the central aspect of our lives. We are lucky that it is fulfilling work—work that we will probably continue to do until we are no longer capable—but it is, unlike that of my parents, all consuming work. There is always an e-mail to answer, a paper or memo to read, and a lecture to give or receive. Success in today's professional world doesn't mean retiring at fifty to play golf in Florida, it means working more and more hours as you move up a towering ladder of economic opportunity (and inequality). Socializing usually revolves around professional colleagues. Not necessarily—or especially—people we actually work with in our own offices. No, most socializing involves weak, work-related ties: folks who are in the same field but just swinging through town for a conference or meeting—potential clients, former mentors, prospective employees. You never know from where the next big project—that great idea—is going to come from in today's "knowledge economy."

In our marriage, nobody cooks. We generally eat take-out,

when I am in charge, or raw food, when my wife is. Whereas, even in my parents' relatively progressive marriage, my mother was the primary caregiver (except for Sundays when my father would take us to Aqueduct Racetrack), in our arrangement it is often more likely that I will be the one to pick up the kids thanks to my wife's more hectic travel schedule. Ours is a constant juggling of iPhone-kept schedules that never quite sync. We try to schedule our commitments so as to always have a free parent to pick up the kids (and in case of emergency). But sometimes it is inevitable that we both have to be away and the decision is whether to make arrangements with my mother or sister to pick them up for a sleepover, or to bring them with us on one or the other of our business trips.

Even when we are both "here" so to speak, we are never quite all here. There's always some distraction. Our cell phones ring, an "urgent" instant message comes in, or perhaps we are just distracted by the million things on that imaginary "to do" list in our minds. And like most professionals today, we don't really produce anything all that tangible. Or, at least, we are so far removed from the production process that sometimes our connection to the stuff around us and the economy in general seems a tad abstract. That doesn't stop us from working, especially when we feel like we are falling behind in relative economic terms—even if, paradoxically, we are faring better than ever in absolute terms.

It's all enough to drive one bonkers. And sometimes I think that is what's happening. Not just to me, but to lots of the folks around me. That rocking chair in my grandparents' house sounds real nice about now. But I can't seem to find it in this Elsewhere Society in which we live.

Elsewhere, U.S.A.

Introduction

Life Among the Elsewhere Class

The alarm clock sounds at 7:00 a.m., and Mr. 1959 rolls out of bed, just as members of the American professional class have been doing for the last hundred years. As he pads down the stairs of his 1,500-square-foot home into a modernized kitchen to pour himself a cup of coffee and read the paper, the house is abuzz with his three kids swirling about, swigging gulps of milk and chomping on freshly buttered toast while gathering up their schoolbooks. His wife is the conductor, orchestrating the scene with her spatula as baton. She reminds the kids that she and Mr. 1959 will be out that evening at their bridge club, but they should not take that as an excuse to forget about their homework.

When the kids have left on their bikes for the public school six blocks away, she serves up a stack of hotcakes to her husband, who shares some of the headlines aloud before checking his wristwatch and realizing he'd better get a move on. So he heads back upstairs to shower, shave, and throw on a suit and tie before strolling out to the carport to drive the station wagon into the city where he works. Now Mrs. 1959 can have coffee with the neighbors, spend an hour or so looking through vacation brochures for their upcoming anniversary trip, and head off to a neighborhood association meeting. She's back to provide snacks by the time the kids arrive home from school.

Meanwhile, at work, Mr. 1959, a newly minted vice president

of a tire company, spends the day on the phone with suppliers of the steel belt that goes into the new radials they are producing. There has been a delay in the latest shipment and the company is at risk of a domino effect of wasted work hours and disgruntled wholesalers if he can't solve the problem; that said, there is little he can do since the only other supplier is in France and the shipping time is too great. Crisis aside, he makes time for a long lunch that includes a couple of drinks. It's his turn to buy: he and his fellow VP from sales always alternate picking up the tab. This is unspoken and fair since they know that they make the same amount of money given their equivalent ranks in the firm.

The alarm clock sounds again, exactly at 7:00 a.m.—only fifty years later. Mr. 2009, a marketing consultant, zaps the button quickly: he has already been up for half an hour and showered—the alarm is really just a safety net. He zips up his $250 jeans and his favorite faux-vintage polyester sweat jacket, faded T-shirt underneath, and gives himself a glance in the mirror. No need to shave—he only does that every third day, preferring the stubbly look (and it's easier on his sensitive skin). Besides, he's just saved himself ten minutes, which he spends scrolling through his BlackBerry to see what messages came in since the last time he checked (at about midnight, a few minutes before he drifted off to sleep, reading material still lying open on his chest).

His wife is probably landing in London now, having taken the red-eye the night before for an afternoon meeting with clients there. She will stay the night in the UK and then fly back the following day. (She *offered* to come back the same day, but Mr. 2009, feeling magnanimous, said he could handle the kids and that she should take a hotel for the night.) So he heads through the condo, grabbing each of the two kids' big toes to shake them awake.

"We'll grab a bagel on the way," he tells them as they rub

sleep from their eyes. In the stainless-steel and granite kitchen, he checks the chart posted on the fridge and adds, "Richard, you have gym today. Wear sneakers. SAT prep at three-thirty and video-making at five. Diane, you've got lacrosse and drama." Richard's barely listening. He sneaks onto Second Life (the virtual online, multiuser domain) and tells his avatar to message friends to meet up online tonight at eight.

During the long SUV drive to their magnet school, Diane realizes she forgot her lacrosse equipment. There's no time to go back, so Mr. 2009 says he'll call one of his interns to run the gear over to her. At the next red light he text-messages the college student to that effect, while his kids chat on their own cell phones. Between dropping them off and reaching his office in the rapidly gentrifying West Thirties, twenty new messages have piled up in his BlackBerry.

He makes a brief appearance at the loftlike office and then heads out to the local Starbucks with his laptop to work on a memo on viral media strategy before his meetings. He finds it hard to concentrate, however, since he can't stop himself from toggling (alt-tab) over to his open-source Firefox browser to e-trade stocks in his self-managed retirement portfolio and search the real estate listings to see how much his neighbors are listing their apartment for. He has been obsessing about the value of his home lately—especially since he and his wife just poured $100K of borrowed money into a renovation.

Sometime around eight in the evening, he and his kids reconvene with their respective laptops at the dining-room banquette that doubles as a meeting table. Japanese food arrives—chicken teriyaki for the kids and sushi for Dad—and Mr. 2009 begins to feel uneasy as the Mexican-born deliveryman peels off his change, dollar by dollar, from the roll of bills he is carrying in the inside pocket of his Windbreaker. He realizes the uneasiness is really guilt. Guilt because this man at his door looks older than the typical delivery person, and for a brief flash he wonders where the man's own kids might be. Guilt because he feels bad that this guy obviously scrapes by on tips, rain or shine, day in and day out, while he pulls down a healthy six figures. So he waves off the man's efforts to hand him his $14 change, telling him it's the tip. But the minute he closes the door, the moral pendulum swings back and he regrets ruining the tip scale for future deliveries.

While they eat, Mr. 2009 asks his kids about their day. They chat as each of them keeps one eye on a computer or other communication device. Dad wishes he could be totally engaged and interested, but he simply can't. It's not just that he is constantly multitasking. It's not just that his attention span seems to have shrunk. It's not just that he is more and more worried about work. It's his kids, too: even if he were totally available, they are not. (It would probably alleviate some of his guilt, though, if he knew that his generation of fathers actually spends more time with their children than any in recent history.)[1]

These two sketches make it clear that a new breed of American has arrived on the scene. This new type of person is a product of contemporary economic and social conditions just as much as William Whyte's "Organization Man" was a product of corporate capitalism in the 1950s. However, the social landscape that gave birth to Mr. and Mrs. 2009—a.k.a. Mr. and Mrs. Elsewhere—bears little resemblance to that of the 1950s, even though the latter still serves as America's common, albeit implicit, reference point. Changes in three areas of our lives— the economy, the family, and technology—have combined to alter the social world and give birth to this new type of American professional. This new breed—the intravidual—has multiple selves competing for attention within his/her own mind, just as, externally, she or he is bombarded by multiple stimuli simultaneously. The necessity of managing these multiple "flows" in a social world where many boundaries have fallen away forms a new ethic for American life. In short, for many of us, *intravidualism* has displaced—or at least competes with—*individualism*. Whereas in American individualism, the ethical imperative was to first find oneself—that is, one's authentic inner core—and then to let that authenticity guide our choices in life, intravidualism is an ethic of managing the myriad data streams, impulses, desires, and even consciousnesses that we experience in our heads as we navigate multiple worlds.

The salient economic trends that have given birth to this new type of American and his way of life include steadily *rising* inequality (between the successful and the very successful) and the intrusion of markets into every nook of our lives. Meanwhile, our family lives have been altered by the wholesale entry of women into the formal labor market (and the associated decline in fertility). And, last, computing and telecommunications technologies have delocalized work for many professionals, so that it can be done at all hours from almost anywhere. No single one of these trends drives the others; in fact, they work together in a forward-feeding system of sorts. Family changes—notably spouses selecting each other for their earning power more than ever before, combined with more working women—actually contribute to the rising inequality, while rising inequality, in turn, drives us to work more (and odder) hours, especially when such work is facilitated by new technologies like wireless computing and BlackBerrys. Of course, the development of such technology is somewhat demand driven by a *need* for flexibility, particularly when professional parents both work. And computerization itself is also a *direct* cause of rising inequality—not to mention the expansion of markets (after all, how could you have eBay, craigslist, or overnight stock trading without the Internet?). As you can see, it is all one big loop that has been spinning forward. Where it will stop, nobody knows.

Not only has the combination of these trends engendered a new breed of person, it has changed the playing field for the rest of us as well. The result is a social world where modernist distinctions like home–office, work–leisure, public–private, and even self–other no longer hold fast. In the twenty-first century, the boundary between work and home has largely disappeared, technological gadgets structure family life, business often intrudes on leisure, inequality creates self-doubt in many of us, and dynamic polygamy (i.e., high rates of relationship formation and dissolution) colors marital relations. Many Americans—particularly those with children to take care of—have morphed into a hyperactive people constantly shuttling between where we think we have to be (home? work? the party full of potential clients?) and where we think we should be (the country for a weekend with the kids? with this husband or a new one?). Those Americans who live in this "Elsewhere Society" are only convinced they're in the right place, doing the right thing, at the right time, when they're on their way to the next destination. Constant motion is a balm to a culture in which the very notion of authenticity—a lodestone of earlier epochs—has been shattered into a thousand e-mails.

Although to some degree all Americans are subject to the forces I've just described, those most intensely affected—the Elsewhere class—are the top third of earners who have children, a professional and monied stratum disproportionately employed in sectors where work can be done at all hours yet no physical product is handled (at least directly, in their immediate midst). I

am speaking of lawyers with young kids at home, and investment bankers, and public relations consultants, and advertising
executives, and yes, overpaid CEOs. The greatest rise in economic inequality has actually, surprisingly, taken place within
this class. The elsewhere phenomenon is by no means universal;
it strikes the younger strata of this class more than the older
ones; parents more than the childless; the urban more than the
rural; and particular personality types more than others.

But who exactly constitutes this new class of American professionals? While there are of course exceptions, in order to qual-
ify as part of the Elsewhere Class, an American must be in the
top half of the income distribution—more likely among the top
fifth, though the line varies by region since the cost of living
does as well. This top stratum owns just over 50 percent of the
nation's wealth.[2] Second, this person must work as a professional
at a job where they do not directly produce a physical product,
but which involves creative, abstract thought—whether that
involves computer code, graphic design, management consult-
ing or leveraged buy-outs. Third, this individual must be hyperconnected: one sign is that she has an Internet-enabled mobile
phone, otherwise known as a smartphone. Lastly, these folks must
have domestic responsibilities in addition to formal ones. My estimate is that somewhere between five to ten percent of the U.S.
adult population below the age of 65 meets these criteria—that
is no less than 9 million and probably no more than 20 million
Americans. Of course, this figure may be growing; furthermore,
since the Elsewhere Class is particularly powerful their values,
norms and preferences exert a disproportionate influence on
society as a whole.

That is, even if we ourselves do not succumb to these forces, we
all may feel their tug on us, or at the very least we witness their
effect on others around us, as well as on the culture writ large.

What has happened to leave so many of us dangling in uncertainty each morning we rise from our beds to manage our multiple selves? A perfect storm—to use a cliché that fits—of economic and household forces. As recently as 1970, the United States enjoyed a robust manufacturing sector: the business of making *stuff.* By contrast, today more than two-thirds of the U.S. economy is service-based—thanks partly to increased efficiency (needing fewer workers to make the same amount of goods) and partly due to off-shoring.[3] Of course, the line between service and manufacturing is often a fuzzy one: If the design engineer draws sketches for the new children's toy, but it is prototyped in Nanjing and stamped out on an assembly line in Mexico, is he providing a service or producing a product? Likewise, if a lawyer draws up the contract for the entire deal to happen, does she work in the "manufacturing" sector? For the purposes of this book, when I talk about service work, I am talking about a range of activities that are abstracted from the construction of a physical product that is consumed. Such activities can range from thinking up new ideas for products to massage therapy to bundling mortgages to moving funds across currencies to take advantage of arbitrage opportunities. As I will explain later, this service economy has made economic relations so highly personalized that the basis for authority under industrial capitalism has withered, often leading to awkward social relations and frequent misunderstandings in a world of work where the lines between business and the personal have blurred.

And as recently as 1990, lights out meant work was finished. But today we can clack away on our BlackBerries in the dark long after our spouses have either fallen asleep from exhaustion or left on the red-eye for an early meeting (while back in the office, huge banks of fluorescent lights remain lit for the janitorial staff working their second job). And work we think we must, since inequality and economic insecurity have risen each year since 1969. The figures on inequality are staggering: Today the richest 10 percent earns five to six times that of the poorest 10 percent.[4] But the real story is at the very top: As the *New York Times* columnist Paul Krugman tells us, "The 13,000 richest families in America had almost as much income as the 20 million poorest households; those 13,000 families had incomes 300 times that of average families."[5]

Not just inequality is on the rise—so is economic insecurity. Today, the risk of a 50 percent income drop from one year to the next is over twice as great for the typical American family as it was in 1970.[6] This is a remarkable change. Thanks to dramatic media attention to selected cases of downsizing the common perception in America is that even white-collar job stability has waned since the glory days of the postwar era.

Such highly publicized layoffs of white-collar employees are a media myth: economists Steven Allen, Robert Clark, and Sylvester Schieber find that average job "tenure and the percentage of employees with 10 or more years of service have actually increased" in large firms, the type that are often spotlighted in news reports.[7] This is due to the fact that white-collar folks disproportionately produce and consume the news media. The truth is that it is—and always has been—those at the bottom who experience the greatest economic insecurity.

That doesn't mean, necessarily, that it is wrong to say that total household income volatility has risen dramatically among professionals. It just means that these economic shocks have less to do with wage cuts or getting fired. The bigger culprit for this class is the increasingly important role of women in the formal labor market. More women are working than ever before, but on average women still maintain a more flexible relationship to paid work. When children are born, for instance, women are likely to reduce their work hours (thereby depressing overall household income). When children reach school age, and especially when they leave the house altogether, women tend to increase their labor supply. What's more, the blackjack-like doubling down effect of high-earning men marrying high-earning women is one of the untold stories contributing to the rise in economic inequality.

Meanwhile, for those at the bottom, high rates of divorce—and even more importantly, the formation and demise of cohabiting relationships—means that you've got a lot of household income drops having nothing to do with employers wielding the ax more often. According to Dr. Jeffrey Timberlake, for example, about a quarter of American children experience two or more mothers' partners by the time they are fifteen![8] Over 8 percent experience three or more maternal domestic partners! That's a lot of earning power coming and going (not to mention emotional turmoil).

Over and above the part that female labor force participation plays in family income fluctuation, the increasingly important role that women play in the economic life of a family forms the bedrock of the real story of middle-class anxiety. That's because household labor—most notably child care—has not gotten any easier in the meantime. Blending work and home responsibilities is no easy feat, especially in a 24/7 service economy that allows many of us to work from home at all hours. One California executive said how great it is to work in his slippers and jeans, do yoga in the middle of the day, and sometimes even make love to his wife. Southern Connecticut is filled with private-equity managers who are able to move billions of dollars of capital at a keystroke while wearing their pajamas. And many say that given how globally and frequently they *do* have to travel when they leave home, it's great to sometimes be able to telecommute instead of trudging into some fluorescently lit office—even if it is a *corner* office.[9] Telecommuting, so to speak, cuts both ways: It allows many professionals with children to work from home. But it also allows many professionals with children to work from home *all the time*. Add in rising inequality across the top half of the income distribution and you've got a recipe for work, work, and more work (this trend, of course, creates more inequality as higher-wage earners work more hours than lower-wage ones). The economist Daniel Hammermesh found, for example, that even when they do the same amount of housework and work the same number of hours at their jobs, it is upper-income women who complain more about a time crunch as compared to their lower-income counterparts.[10] That is, when you can earn more per hour, the opportunity cost of *not* working feels greater and the pressure is all the more intense.

Another myth is that Americans are moving around more than ever. In fact, while we travel more for leisure and business and commute longer distances to work, we are actually relocating less often than we did in previous eras. In a study titled "Ever More Rooted Americans," the sociologist Claude Fisher shows that the percentage of Americans who moved in 2000 (about 17 percent) is 3 points lower than the 20 percent who moved in 1950.[11] So the story of the mobile creative class hopping from San Francisco to Austin, Texas, to Massachusetts's I-90 corridor is perhaps one for young adults—if at all. Once we have children, some of us change partners more than we change locations. Upper-class jet-setters may do business across the globe, but they are increasingly rooted in their home lives.*

---

*In fact, it is lower-income Americans who have experienced a slight rise in moving, even as the overall rates have declined. (See Claude Fisher, "Ever-More Rooted Americans," *City & Community* 1 [June 2002]: 174–94.)

Homeownership is, perhaps, the real reason—having risen from 43.6 percent in 1940[12] to 68.1 percent in 2007.[13] (Who knows how many additional divorces are prevented thanks to the difficulty of liquidating the family home? Or how many are caused by the foreclosure crisis?)

This rise in homeownership, in turn, may itself be a source of anxiety for several reasons. First, when you rent, you don't have to think twice before pouring some glob down the drain. After all, it's not you who has to pay for the plumber if it stops up. Homeowning, in other words, creates a lot of hassles with which we have to deal on a fairly regular basis. Second, while homeownership has historically proven to be a good investment, especially when you figure in the money saved from not renting, it does entail a fair bit of risk and worry. Risk with respect to the value of your home. And worry in that you have to constantly be figuring out whether you should refinance, add on, renovate, take out a home equity line of credit, and so on. No longer is the home a haven from the business world. Now the family home is a potential profit (and loss) center, too.

The sum total of these trends is that even in good times when Americans are doing better than ever before—especially those lucky enough to be in the top half—many of them think they are falling behind. For example, when the *New York Times* conducted a poll in Manhattan—the most unequal county in the United States—it found that upper-income folks ($200K+) were almost twice as likely as those with lower incomes to say that "seeing other people with money" made them feel poor.[14]

Something is new here. Ever-striving Americans in a land of immigrant dreams and Horatio Alger myths is nothing remarkable on this continent. What is novel is that Americans used to work themselves to the bone for material necessities and to rise up out of constant struggle *so their children wouldn't have to.* Leisure was something you attained when you reached a certain income level. Today, a different dynamic has taken shape: For the first time in history, the more we are paid, the more hours we work. Paradoxically, perhaps, we do this now because among the luckiest of us the rewards for working are so great, they make the "opportunity cost" of not working all the greater. The result is that we no longer have leisure-class elites. The rich are working harder than ever. (Even those born to great wealth now feel the pressure to work for work's sake.) Rather, leisure is something for the poor. This seemingly arcane economic measure—the income elasticity of leisure—represents a fundamental change in how many of us live; and, obviously, this change has affected not just when we work, but also how we play, how we love, how we raise our children—how we live.[15]

Of course, there will always be those folks who cut against the grain. Those who—despite the Wharton M.B.A. and all the student loans it took to acquire—choose to spend their days at the beach surfing, drive an old beater car, and organize spontaneous games of ultimate Frisbee on the weekends. But they may acutely feel that they are swimming against strong social currents and economic undertows. So much so that sometimes such efforts to preserve tradition become so self-aware, so hyperconsciously pursued as to defeat their own purpose. The point is that even the same action—say playing catch with one's kid on a Saturday afternoon—takes on a different meaning because the entire social playing field has shifted beneath the feet of those ballplayers. That is, you can never go home again. Even the same cherished rituals and actions may evoke very different emotions given the new context in which they are situated.

So, it's not hard to understand why so many apparently successful Americans are suffering from what we sociologists used to call *alienation*. An old term, to be sure, but one that I think needs to be revived. It's the best one-word definition of the sense many of the folks in this striving, monied class have that they present themselves as one person but are really another; that we carry alongside ourselves a kind of mirror self (or selves) in which our reflections always differ slightly from the "real" thing. In these strata, many are dogged by an increased disconnect between how they expect to feel—when they get a big promotion, when they interact with a colleague, when they buy something online, when they hang out with their kids at the beach—and how they actually feel. And though the most objective statistics indicate that they are doing better than ever before, these professionals still feel more nervous, work harder, and even sleep less (or so they claim to survey takers—I'm skeptical that this is not a new sort of bragging) than at any time in American history. Driven by a phantom anxiety that something big is going to go wrong, the most successful professional class in the most powerful country in the world lives in fear that its personal house of economic cards is about to collapse. Maybe that's why, while drinking has declined, adult use of other mind-altering substances such as Valium or marijuana has risen to the point where mature adults consume more than teenagers for the first time since such trends were first tracked.[16]

I believe I may be describing some folks you know. They—and how they live today—are what this book is about. There's plenty to examine. For, in 2009, their triumphs are often followed by an aftertaste of disappointment—seeded by either the nagging feeling they don't deserve it or, conversely, that the accolade indicates the low standards of the bestower. Many of this new breed of intraviduals feel stressed out and dislocated from both home and work responsibilities. Since, for almost all of their great efforts, most professionals produce nothing tangible at their place of work, many can frequently feel like frauds. Hence the constant fear among many folks that they're one misstep away from being "found out." And all this in a culture that has blended work and leisure ethics to such a degree that there is actually a meta-pressure to *not* appear stressed out. They have to get that report done and the kids off to school. But they also have to look cool while they are multitasking, as if they were teenagers who didn't want to get caught studying for the big test lest they be called eggheads.

An earthquake in the social landscape is not quite the right metaphor for what has happened to us. A better analogy is global warming: In their slow and steady march, these socioeconomic trends (and the new breed of person they have engendered) have invisibly crept upon us like rising CO_2 concentrations in the atmosphere. The alteration to the social landscape has been a slow accretion by degrees, much the same way a city evolves from a patch of primordial forest. No one moment marks the change from totally rural to completely urban, but before we know it, our world is different, and we may wonder how we got here. Or we may only be able to retain a vague notion that things somehow used to be different. We might even confuse these feelings with the nostalgia for our own individual youth with which they mingle. But they are indeed distinct from youthful nostalgia in that the loss has been collective rather than individual.

The present story will not focus on isolated economic trends in themselves—there are already plenty of books out there which do that. Rather, I seek to explain how these trends have combined to give rise to a new type of American and to a new texture of everyday life. This kind of narrative is only possible now. While we were being born into this new era, such selves-understanding was not possible. But now that birth is over and the new epoch is here—and here to stay. And we must begin the process of making sense of it.

From the Protestant Ethic
to the Elsewhere Ethic

W e all know we are on some new wild ride. We may have all made mental notes to ourselves to slow down, examine our (multiple) lives, and take stock of what has happened—but, of course, we don't have time to reflect. However, we all know the symptom quite well—there is a palpable sense out there that many of us have lost control of our lives. Mr. and Mrs. Elsewhere feel like they need to be not just in two places at once but literally everywhere at the same time.

In a nutshell, what has happened is that many boundaries that were the hallmarks of industrial capitalism—investment v. consumption; private sphere v. public space; price v. value; home v. office; leisure v. work; boss v. employee; and ultimately, even self v. other—have become blurred and interpenetrating.

This sense of unease has been made worse since the speed of change has left us with no chance to recalibrate expectations and arrive at a fresh social paradigm. Each economic epoch must—in good time—come to an ideological equilibrium of sorts. In America prior to the 1930s, that equilibrium was best explained by *The Protestant Ethic and the Spirit of Capitalism* (1920). In this classic text, Max Weber argued that the key to the development of market capitalism was the emergence of a new moral paradigm. In medieval Catholic Europe, poverty was a virtue, and to profit off one's fellow man was considered evil. But the Protestant Reformation and its association of earthly riches with heavenly salvation changed all that, and, Weber argued, acted as the engine of capitalist growth. Protestantism in general—and Puritanism in particular—eliminated the formal structure of the Church and paved the way for a one-to-one relationship with God. This resulted in an enormous amount of spiritual insecurity: How do I know that I am saved if there is no priest—no sacred rite—to guarantee it? The answer lay in appearing blessed by living an ascetic life, working hard, and accumulating lots of money. Success as salvation created a very effective incentive structure. The individual controlled his worldly enterprise and was given spiritual options that vested in the afterlife.

However, the Great Depression, the New Deal, and the rise of trade unionism eclipsed the Protestant Ethic somewhere around the middle of the last century. The newfound wealth of a globally dominant U.S. economy allowed for a truce between expansive corporate America and organized labor such that a communitarian ethos could reign supreme. Books like Whyte's *Organization Man* or David Reisman's *The Lonely Crowd* attest to this change in the social character of 1950s America.

There has always been an uneasy compromise between the individual and community life in America. And the fundamental tension in midcentury American society was thus the tension between individualism and conformity—between, on one hand, the heroic entrepreneur who amasses personal wealth, and on the other hand, the loyal corporate soldier. The Protestant Ethic valued thrift over consumption, work over leisure, and opportunism over loyalty. But the large bureaucratic organizations like IBM, GM, and RCA that dominated the social landscape in the 1950s put a premium on teamwork, compromise, and fealty. To get ahead in the corporation, the "Organization Man" needed to work long hours and yet also conform to the "social ethic" of newly suburbanized America by "belonging." He had to fit into the group, not outshine its members. The best way to fit in was to consume: to buy, buy, buy, even if on credit—something unthinkable to the nineteenth-century entrepreneur. But a new social ethic never totally eclipses the previous one—leading to tensions and strains in the economy and its accompanying culture.

Today, those midcentury tensions have been resolved, this time through redefinition: Leisure is work and work is leisure. Consumption is investment. A tax-deductible home equity loan is savings. And the salience of social connections does not indicate nepotism but rather social capital and entrepreneurial skill totally consistent with meritocratic ideals. The corporation has widened and flattened, resolving many of the tensions between sociability and hierarchy. Loyalty has been replaced by value: Indeed, you show your value within the organization through calculated displays of *dis*loyalty—that is, by leveraging outside offers from other corporate suitors. Even our religion has undergone a transformation: Lately, the ideology of the Protestant Ethic has been stood on its head. Now the fastest-growing churches are those that completely reverse Weber's formula. Rather than doing well economically in order to get a sign that one is saved, a new breed of churches espouses an ethic that promises worldly riches if you find salvation. That is, in the Amway Church or Reverend Creflo A. Dollar's 25,000-member Atlanta congregation, parishioners pray for salvation *so that* they can get rich.

But resolving the conflicts of midcentury America has exacted its own terrible price: the fragmentation of the self, not to mention alienation and anxiety among today's professional classes—those Americans who earn lots of money but who need to work for it. The 24/7, dual-sex information economy in which they work—riddled with inequality between the rich and the very rich—has changed the way we do business, advance our careers, and navigate our personal lives. This socioeconomic restructuring has generated wide reverberations perhaps best illustrated by three discrete (if interrelated) phenomena: the economic red shift; the portable workshop; and the price culture. These three phenomena combine to create the Elsewhere Ethic that haunt Mr. and Mrs. 2009, giving rise to a sense of alienation among them and many of their professional colleagues. Let me explain.

Though, on paper, many professionals in America are doing better than ever before, rising inequality in the top half of the distribution chain has created a sense of panic even in good times. I call this an economic red shift since it is not the high levels of inequality per se that are key, but the ever-rising trend that matters: From any link in the chain, it looks like everyone else is rushing away. We may be doing better and pulling away from those below us (perhaps that old college friend who is still struggling to find his calling), while the folks just above us on the income ladder are leaving us in their wake. Like the Doppler effect—the red shift in the galactic light spectrum that is induced by the expansion of the universe and can be observed from any point—an individual in the top half of income distribution appears, to herself, to be at the eye of an economic storm. This is equally true for those in the top 1 percent as for those just above the median U.S. income. This simultaneous dropping of the floor and raising of the ceiling is enough to induce a panicked, though rational, anxiety response: Work constantly.

Such a response is abetted by the fact that we *can* work constantly—in our personal portable workshop. I've borrowed this image from the medieval craftsman who fashioned products one by one in his own cottage industry. This craftsman set his own hours as he was paid for piecework. However, there were inherent limits to how much he could work. He needed raw materials. He needed light (so was generally confined to working during the day). And he needed customers (limited to a very local market). But today's professional in the knowledge economy is uninhibited by pesky materials or the need to work with specific implements in a "shop." She can work at any and all times, as long as she has an outlet to plug into and a decent wireless connection. In the flexible nature of the post-industrial economy, this new professional shares the freedom of the medieval craftsman to draw up her own schedule, but she is driven by the economic red shift to work any and all hours, made possible by the portable workshop of the BlackBerry and the laptop.

Finally, we all live in a price culture, a world where those meals that used to be free on airlines now have an explicit cost. Many economists would say that pricing the formerly priceless is a step in the right direction since it enhances efficiency. Why should I subsidize the guy in the seat next to me when he asks for three extra bags of pretzels, and I am content with one? By making that cost explicit, I ostensibly get to pay a lower base fare. What's more, pricing the formerly unpriced brings many once shadowy relationships out in the open. Where prices are not explicit, there lurks the potential for exploitation. Think about hidden fees in credit cards. The more explicit such costs are, the better informed the consumer is, and the more we can make good choices for ourselves.

This would all be fine and dandy if there were no transaction costs—that is, costs inherent in just enforcing such fairness and efficiency. And it would be okay if it stopped at lousy airline food and other "stuff." But pricing the formerly priceless has spread to every nook and cranny of our lives, thereby eroding other sorts of economies. When we move to price marriage (through divorce settlements or prenups) or physical comfort (by paying masseuses) or even a friendly ear (through psychotherapy), we destroy the desire, need, and ability to exchange such "priceless" things through nonmarket channels, and we thereby add to our sense of alienation from one another. Of course, sometimes these market-based relationships can expose us to folks we might not otherwise have met; and these contacts can, in turn, evolve into nonmarket relationships: The buyer for a large department store ends up marrying the sales rep for the fashion designer. Wonderful! The patient runs off with the therapist. *Wonderful?* Besides obvious conflicts of interest, one problem with working backward from market to nonmarket relationships is that intimacy and trust can be very difficult to construct on the foundation of an erstwhile business relationship—not to mention the havoc to professional norms that office romance often wreaks.

This pricing also feeds into the paradoxes of an economy that produces no material goods—a "stuffless" economy—since we really can't know how price relates to value for many services. That's thanks to two factors. First, many things we buy today have zero marginal cost. For example, when I download an audiobook from Audible.com, the *additional* (or marginal) cost to Audible or the publisher is close to nil as compared to a physical copy of a book, which costs additional paper, binding, printing, and shipping. Classic economic theory tells us that price should equal marginal cost in a competitive market. Of course, there has never been a pure market as described in Econ 101; but only in this totally dematerialized product setting do we approach a situation where the marginal cost of selling one more of something truly approaches zero. The price-value ratio, then, seems elusive. But, at least on the retail side, we can assess how much we enjoyed the product and how much use we got out of it.

However, the situation is even worse for big corporate trans-

actions. Here the problem relates to the second factor: a difficulty in assessing the impact of a service purchased. By way of
example, I was recently on an American Airlines flight when the
flight attendant announced all the snack items for sale (items
which, of course, used to be free). She wrapped up her soliloquy
by declaring that now, "American Airlines is happy to accept
American Express or other major credit cards." Clearly, Amex
and AA had struck some sort of deal: American Express was
paying the airline some undisclosed amount to be singled out in
the credit card announcement. How many memos must have
gone back and forth to cut that deal? How many billable attorneys' hours? How many training sessions for the flight staff?

And how much should Amex have paid for this privilege?
Should they have gotten a discount since the first word of their
brand is also the first word of American Airlines and thereby
reinforces—albeit in a subtle way—the host company's image?
In order to know the value of the deal, they would have had to
know how much the marketing campaign increases their business. Impossible. No focus group or statistical model will tell
Amex how much worse or better their bottom line would have
been in the absence of this marketing campaign. Ditto for the
impact of billboards, product placement, and special promotions
like airline mileage plans. There are simply too many other
forces that come into play to be able to isolate the impact of a
specific effort. Ditto for most of the symbolic economy.

It is ironic that in this age of markets and seemingly limitless information, we can't get the very answers we need to
make rational business decisions. Value is elusive in our economy. Often we are just guessing. So our own worth is therefore
elusive, too. Anxiety about that worth is thus a rational response,
as is our suspicion that we may be frauds. The real estate agent
knows that a savvy consumer can see the same listings online

that he has access to and must constantly justify his "value added." The lawyer knows that 99 percent of the contracts she draws up are themselves 99 percent boilerplate language, and in a pinch the paralegal who typed it can actually double-check it and file it in court, for that matter. The M.D.-certified ophthalmologist knows that the immigrant, community-college-educated technician could probably manage computerized Lasix eye surgery as well as he could, if not better (and, in fact, does perform much of the procedure). The anxious college professor knows how much she *doesn't* know as she stands up to give her lecture. To top it off, she also worries that everything she *does* know her students can find fairly easily with the help of Wikipedia, Google, iTunes U, and a little entrepreneurial spirit. And the public affairs officer of the major corporation knows that all her job boils down to is the hocking of exclusives that are created by generating false scarcities of information—something that she could impart to her replacement in about fifteen minutes.

This constant fear of being exposed, cut out, or outsourced, and thereby having one's "capital" rendered valueless, is the principal pathos of the era. Not everyone suffers from it. But we can all recognize it in people around us; it is so rife that the *Harvard Business Review* devotes articles to dealing with fraud anxiety among executives. "Many skilled, accomplished executives fear that they're not good enough—impostors about to be found out," Manfred de Vries writes in the *HBR* article that was voted third best for 2005. "By undervaluing their talent, are they ruining their careers and companies?"[1] When you can't assess yourself, when you're unsure of your place in the world, what you end up feeling is alienation, a sense that we have lost control over the rhythm and content of our daily lives—not to mention a nagging feeling that we need to be somewhere else.

OF COURSE, THAT KIND OF FEELING IS NOT NEW . . .

Way back in 1867, in the heyday of the Industrial Revolution, Karl Marx (yes, that Karl Marx) wrote all about how capitalism instilled alienation among workers. It was a different time, but in many ways his four dimensions of alienation still apply. According to Marx, Mr. 19th Century was alienated first from the very product he produced: By virtue of the factory's division of labor, he could only know a fraction of what it actually took to make the whole (who, for example, knows how to make an entire motorcycle from scratch except the Fonz on *Happy Days*?). Mr. 1867 was alienated next from the process of labor: Unavoidable, since, unlike Marx's idealized medieval craftsman, the factory worker could not set his own schedule and work rhythm but had to answer to the time clock and the wagemaster. Alienated from the labor process and product, it thus was inevitable that he was also alienated from himself: The act of creation that had made him uniquely human was no longer possible (never mind that recent studies have shown that chimps are tool creators as well). Finally, he was alienated from other people, since capitalism makes all relations market relations.

Mrs. and Mr. Elsewhere are also alienated from their products. The intangibility of the new economy means that we never have a sense of having produced a single actual thing. The "satisfaction" of having earned a 15 percent return for one's clients or written the language for the contract of the leveraged buyout or talked the patient through their neuroses simply cannot substitute for the leather shoe or wooden chair that we once fashioned with our own hands. In today's economy, many are dogged by the question, "What was my value added?" Even when there is a resulting physical product, Mr. 2009 is generally so far removed from the site of its fabrication that he may question the relationship between his labor and the resulting output. The anxious CEO, attorney, architect, or hedge fund manager can, of course, always point to the price that was paid for her services in the marketplace as a proxy for her value. But ultimately, this is cold comfort since there is a moral dimension to value, too, as indicated by the double entendre of the word itself. We once held the collective belief that there were some things money couldn't buy (before MasterCard deployed the oxymoronic ad campaign that co-opted the phrase). Even among things we did bring to and from the marketplace in exchange for cash, we had a sense of their worth. Hence the notion of getting a good deal (or a poor one)—that is, a recognition that price didn't always reflect "true" worth. That division between price and value has increasingly collapsed under the weight of economic rationality that spreads like wildfire across sectors of our existence, leaving alienation in its wake.

The new breed of modern professional is, like his ninteenth-century factory worker counterpart, also alienated from his labor, only in a more subtle way perhaps. Because we have flex-time, Mr. and Mrs. 2009 experience a paradox: Like the medieval craftsman, they are free to set their own hours, go to lunch when they please, work from home or the road—all seemingly liberating trends; but unlike the craftsman, they are continuously dogged by work. The medieval guildsman might have experienced a sense of completion when he finished off a week's worth of orders. And, of course, the midcentury manager in a big corporation could always have written another memo or visited another factory. But the sheer speed of telecommunications was always a limiting factor—until now. There is a constancy that is new: Mrs. Elsewhere can't escape her e-mail, voice mail, expense reports, and so on. This constant linkage is exacerbated by the fact that each e-mail to which she successfully responds will generate, in turn, another two requiring attention. And any of this can be done at any time of the day or night. It is not just that there is more work to do, but that it is unconstrained by place and time. Thus, work becomes the engine and the person the caboose, despite all this so-called freedom and efficiency.

Take my wife, Natalie Jeremijenko. A design engineer, she has felt compelled to embrace the newest information technologies. During the 1990s, she traveled in the backseat of the car on family trips with her laptop humming, the power cord hooked into the cigarette lighter, and a black metal rectangular box clipped onto the screen, dashing off e-mails in real time while chatting on another black boxlike cell phone. The laptop clip-on was called "Ricochet," a product that used radio networks to provide linkage to the Internet as we sped through California's Santa Clara Valley before the advent of GPRS (Internet service) on BlackBerries and Treos. A few years later, she became an early adopter of Skype—the Internet-based phone system—so that she could video-conference with Australia (her home continent), the UK, and Belgium about various projects. When our son would wet his bed, he would wander out to a blazingly lit living room to find his mother discussing project proposals for cageless zoos, color-coded interactive parking lots, and upside-down tree plantings with various collaborators around the globe. Scheduling appointments at 3:00 a.m. was not an uncommon practice. And since she was traveling so much, 3:00 a.m. in New York may just have been 9:00 a.m. in the time zone to which she had most recently been acclimated.

"M—O—M!" he would yell, having taken a liking to spelling and acronyms. "Come cuddle me." She would hold up a finger, asking him to wait a moment as she explained how students could upload their visual essays documenting the manufacturing practices of their chosen product to her "How Stuff Is Made" (www.howstuffismade.org) Wiki site. The conversation with Europe would drag on too long, however, even after she said she had to go. Finally, the five-year-old would slam down the Mac, causing it to immediately hibernate and thereby cutting off the transatlantic connection. M-O-M would come to bed, nestling S-O-N in the dry parental sheets. She'd doze off for a few hours before starting the next day.

Today, with fully equipped iPhone in hand, Natalie's work is more efficient than ever, and, as if in an escalating arms race, our children have developed strategies of varying effectiveness to get the attention they want and need, from taking away her computer to grabbing her face in both hands and swiveling her gaze to theirs with all the control of an experienced barber. But her heart still breaks when our daughter asks why she can't just stay home like all the other mothers. Natalie loves her work, but she constantly feels overwhelmed by it, as if her very work were an abusive, oppressive boss screaming at her. Listening to my daughter's question, though, I can't help pointing out that Natalie is now the norm and not the exception. After all, whereas in the 1950s, 17 percent of women with children worked outside the home, today, over 68 percent do.[2] These multitasking mothers have reshaped many of our norms and boundaries regarding home and work life.

I could also not help wondering what difference it would make whether Natalie stayed at home since the kids themselves were pretty booked up all day long anyway. For we certainly keep our kids busy—nearly as busy as we are ourselves. Every second is an opportunity for investment in their human and cultural capital—that is, in their cognitive and noncognitive skill sets. Our kids are not playing; rather, they are learning to socialize with peers. They are not mashing clay; they are developing their manipulative dexterity in a three-dimensional medium. They are not kicking the ball around; no, they are physically challenging their fine and gross motor skills. They aren't just playing soccer, they are learning to function in rule-based systems and interact with nonparental institutional authority figures (a.k.a. the coaches). It would be odd enough if these were all just the same activities with new labels, and sometimes they are, but often they are not. How we interact and what we do have actually changed. I call how we spend our time (I would say "free" time, but that would obscure the point that this once hallowed boundary has broken down) *instrumental leisure* or *weisure* (i.e., work and leisure combined), since the info-economy puts a premium on quk, shrt trms tht cn b txtd fst & rmmbrd easily.

And what we are doing during our weisure time is accumulating social capital and developing our networks. Seen as a shortcut to the top that flew in the face of meritocratic ideals back during the social ethic of the 1950s, networking through weisure is now a skill that Americans pay millions of dollars to book publishers and network trainers to cultivate. This is not false consciousness, either. Social capital is real capital in the information economy. Those who control social valves—connections between individuals—are the ones who are able to profit through information arbitrage.

That's why Mr. Elsewhere is constantly having "meetings" that are ambiguous in nature. Part of each workday is spent drinking lattes with folks who may be potential clients, or investors, or just interesting people from whom the newest hot idea for private equity may arise. Since one never knows where the next next big thing is lurking, any meeting could result in the opportunity of a lifetime for the artist, movie producer, venture capitalist, salesperson, or business consultant. It could be the woman he meets on the plane who runs an environmental non-profit that badly needs a Web redesign. It could be the father of his child's playmate in the sandbox who runs a hedge fund on his BlackBerry while changing dirty diapers. Or it could even be the kid herself, who has just the look Mrs. 2009 needs for her newest marketing campaign. Even when the Elsewhere class ostensibly go out purely to socialize, they find that they cannot stop themselves from glancing at their text messages, talking work, or making valuable introductions across the table. It all may be a Ponzi scheme, but it certainly is no shell game: In an information and service economy, much of what drives success is, in fact, social skills.

This new merger between work and play can even be seen in the names of the giant corporations that now dominate our business world. Whereas in industrial capitalism the monikers of corporate behemoths attempted to connote nationalism, grandeur, and heaviness, in the new info-economy, playfulness is paramount. Google replaces U.S. Steel; Napster trumps General Motors; and Wikipedia beats out *Encyclopaedia Britannica*. One has trouble imagining the General Standard Search Engine, just as Yahoo! Oil Industries sounds a little off.

Even our kids have gotten into the "game," so to speak. When we are not programming their time to develop their fine motor skills, they retreat to the online Shangri-La of Club Penguin, Neopets, and Webkinz. These and other online games popular among the elementary school set have begun to train children for their future. That is, much of their video game "play" entails doing jobs—such as making pizzas or unloading trucks (physical labor)—to earn "coins" or "Neopet points" in order to buy virtual objects online for their two-dimensional pets.

This work-and-play blurring ends up enhancing Mrs. and Mr.

Elsewhere's sense of alienation: It's not just that they feel like they need to be working when they are ostensibly supposed to be having fun or, conversely, that they should stop working and be there for their kids, spouse, or friends. It's not just that Mr. and Mrs. 2009 need to be everywhere at once. It's that the once disparate spheres have now collided and interpenetrated each other, creating a sense of "elsewhere" at all times. I'm not just talking about the increase in travel and telecommunications, I am talking about the more subtle changes that they have rendered: the fact that home is more like work and work is more like home and that the private and public spheres are increasingly indistinguishable from each other.

Also in line with the elsewhere business ethic is the collapse of the consumption/investment dichotomy. That is, just as leisure is work and work is leisure (i.e., weisure), so, too, consumption equals investment. A tax-deductible home equity loan is savings. Though it costs 50 to 100 grand to redo a kitchen with Miele appliances and a Sub-Zero refrigerator, these are really investments, we tell ourselves, since the data show that kitchen and bathroom remodeling typically retain 97 percent of their cost during resale. Ditto for the house—or McMansion—itself, which has more than doubled in size since the 1950s. Likewise, the Hummer is tax-deductible (since it is classified not as a car but as a light truck). Not to mention the time-share in the private jet (ostensibly for business use—wink, wink). Even the bacchanal thrown by *Wired* magazine—replete with custom martinis and corporate goodie bags—is really an investment in customer relations. Consumption is redefined as investment, as all these expenses are seen as the cost of doing business. And as long as business or the real estate market is chugging briskly along, they do perhaps pay for themselves—even if they require a second mortgage to finance. In short, everything is tax-deductible, even if the IRS would not agree. This is the new form of spending, what I'll call *convestment*—the sometimes rocky marriage of consumption and investment.

We can also see this new form of spending, for instance, in the rise of gambling as a recreational activity. Today betting losses represent one-quarter of personal consumer expenditures, up from 5 percent in 1970.[3] Who would have thought that trying to make money—against the odds stacked in the house's favor, no less—was a relaxing way to spend our time away from the rat race? Likewise, one of the most popular forms of gambling, slot machines, involves the seemingly mind-numbing action of inserting a small metal disk into a slot and then pulling a lever. Something that would have epitomized the dullness of Taylorized work in the bygone industrial age is now the way we "get into a zone" of privacy, becoming one with the machine, and escape the oppressive sociality of the service sector and the mind-bending tasks associated with the knowledge economy. Whereas pulling the lever of the machine was once the gesture that clocked you in and out of work, that very same motion now symbolizes our escape from the oppressive sociality of work.[4]

This remerger of work and play is quite ironic, since some theorists of industrial capitalism saw the emergence of the modern market as the very thing that allowed for a sacrosanct private sphere. That is, it was through the market's ethic of the separation of business and pleasure that a "private sphere" in which economic relations were verboten was created for the first time in history with modern capitalism. "Neither a borrower nor a lender be" and "Don't do business with friends" are just two of the maxims that illustrate this social norm. Such a cleavage stood in stark contrast to economic life in prior epochs. Back in Renaissance Florence, for example, your neighbor might supply your raw materials for your blacksmith business, not to mention being the person to whose daughter you married off your only son. These cross-purpose relationships created a high degree of uncertainty and a potential for distrust. (Think of the Mafia today.) He could be bilking you on the price of iron, but what could you really say about it since you dine together regularly? Or, it could be that you found better-quality charcoal across town, but how could you tell your neighbor to keep his charcoal (and his daughter)? (Alternatively, on another occasion when you are in a more magnanimous mood, you could be reassured that you are getting a good deal because you are part of the same extended family.) Only when a monetized market had developed where there were clear prices for everything could all of this resentment be avoided and purely personal ties emerge. For example, some optimists might argue that with the economic necessity of marriage declining—thanks to the increasing financial independence of women—conjugal relations can now flourish as a purely private choice relationship, based on shared interests, passions, and affinities.

That's all well and nice, except that by now we have come full circle: The formerly private sphere has become so commoditized by the ever-expanding marketplace that literally everything has a price. We know the value of watching our kids, and our ailing parents, since many of us hire other folks to do it for us. We know the price of cleaning a toilet bowl, if we have ever hired a cleaning service. We know the value of a soft touch or caress, since we can walk into many beauty salons and order a massage in fifteen-minute increments. And we know the value of a good friend who will listen to you, since some of us pay for it in the form of psychotherapy or a life coach. We know the value of our own marriages since we increasingly make it explicit in the form of divorce settlements (or prenuptial agreements, which, though still rare, are on the rise).[5] We even put a price on our very lives, since we buy insurance in case they end too soon or annuities in case they last too long. There is little that one could imagine needing done that can't be outsourced to the marketplace. A brief glance at Craig's List illustrates the pervasiveness of market rationalities. Not only can you systematize your search for a life partner or casual sexual encounter, but you can also find a meditative body work consultant, a mover, a lawyer, a Tarot card reader who makes house calls, someone to care for your elderly grandmother, someone to struggle through homework with your kids, a yoga consultant, even an ovum whose previous owner scored high on her SATs, or, alternatively, someone to carry your own ovum.

Market conquest used to be spatial, that is, global in scale. With periodic crises of capitalism—economic downturns—we continually needed to find new places to sell our "stuff." Hence colonialism, which solved the problems of finding raw materials *and* new customers (not to mention cheap labor). Now, with intellectual property laws (key to the new economy) difficult to enforce in emerging markets, a sort of internal colonization is taking place. By internal colonization, I mean that whereas once we sailed the seas in search of new markets for our products and new sources of raw materials and labor, now we do this increasingly domestically by expanding the sheer number and type of markets. Whether embodied by the rise of the bottled-water industry and its displacement of public drinking fountains, or the proliferation of nannies, personal trainers, and assistants, or the ability to sell family memorabilia on eBay, money and market relations have eroded barriers that once maintained the sanctity and clarity of private space.

In this way, the networked service economy has borne out in spades Marx's prediction about social relations becoming market relations and creating a new form of alienation. After all, how can we trust the therapist who tells us we need to go from one to two sessions a week since it is in her financial interest for us to come more often? How can we be confident our primary care physician has our best interests at heart, not the HMO's bottom line, when he tells us that we don't need additional tests? But it's not just trust that is damaged. Thanks to the market's invasion of every aspect of our lives, many social ties have become fleeting and one-dimensional. That is, unlike preindustrial societies, most of those professionals we interact with in an average day are service people fulfilling just one specific function in our lives, a function for which we pay them. So the individual that professionals pay to raise their children is generally not the same person they pay to listen to their problems or to work out the knots in their necks. This makes modern social life extremely fragile; for if Mr. 2009 runs out of cash, how will he get his needs fulfilled? Once you have outsourced such fulfillment to the marketplace, there is little hope of a backrub on credit or a sympathetic ear from a therapist who hasn't been paid by your insurance company for months. Perhaps more critically, this dynamic contributes to the intravidualism phenomenon by fragmenting and dispersing one's attentions— physical, emotional, familial. And as we all know, it's hard to put something back together once it has shattered into a million pieces.

The next chapter details the concrete changes that led us little by little from the social ethic of the 1950s to the Elsewhere Ethic of intravidualism today. As we shall see, there is no one trend— the rise of computers, increasing female labor force participation, suburbanization—that can get us from there to here. Just as it is the intersection of the economic red shift, the portable workshop, and the price society—and not any of these alone— that creates this new social landscape, so it is a series of parallel and interrelated historical steps that has fundamentally altered the everyday experience of many professionals in America over the last fifty years.

And You May Find Yourself
Behind the Wheel of a Large Automobile

From General Motors to Google

While the daily rhythms and experiences of Mr. 1959 and Mr. 2009 feel vastly different, it is also true that Mr. 1959 is the symbolic father of today's new breed of professional, for it was the social, technological, and economic arrangements of the 1950s that gave birth to those of today—if often in unintended ways. Back in the day, the scholar Daniel Yergin called the worker-consumer of the mid-twentieth-century "Hydrocarbon Man." Hydrocarbon Man—an acceptable alternative to my Mr. 1959—was the quintessential citizen of the Oil Century (another name for Henry Luce's "American Century"). In 1949 (the year that the social critic Naohiro Amaya claimed marked the beginning of the Oil Century), two thirds of the world's energy was provided by coal. By 1973, oil had replaced coal in the top spot, satisfying more than half of global energy needs.[1]

According to Amaya, Karl Marx and other nineteenth-century critics of capitalism had written during the age of coal. Coal was and remains dirty and difficult to extract.* Coal-fired factories during the Industrial Revolution required huge amounts of this fuel, which, in turn, was very labor-intensive and dangerous to retrieve. Many workers literally fed the huge machine. The lives of coal miners—or factory workers, for that

*Never mind that with global reserves dwindling, oil is now increasingly dirty and difficult to extract.

matter—were difficult and dangerous. Hence labor relations were more often than not combative and violent. Fear of labor conflict—and its tendency to slow or block production—was one reason why America switched over from coal to oil as its primary source of fuel.

By displacing coal, oil in turn allowed for a whole new lifestyle for workers, best embodied by the family car. Now, instead of one huge machine (the nineteenth-century factory), we had evolved to a situation where oil-powered, small-scale machines were everywhere. Rather than hundreds of individuals traveling in the belly of one machine (the locomotive train), now each individual had her own, almost monogamous relationship with her automobile. Rather than being dominated and alienated by huge modern technologies of our own creation, as Marx had claimed, we were now back in the driver's seat, quite literally. The expansion of the electrical grid allowed for lots of little machines —otherwise known as home appliances—to dot our lives as well. Oil-powered motors and machines came to replace not just coal-powered devices (such as the home furnace) but also manual-powered devices. Hence the invention of the electric can opener. The Mixmaster replaces the eggbeater; the Cuisinart augments the chopping board; and so on. Of course, the ultimate machine turned out to be the computer, but we will get to that in due time.

This midcentury revolution in power combined with the postwar hunger for new products to produce a seller's market in the ensuing economic boom. For example, William Levitt (of Levittown fame) had to pay a $1,000 premium (about half the sticker price) to secure a Nash automobile for his mother. Not to worry: He, in turn, enjoyed long waiting lists of families desperate to buy his houses in the suburban communities of single-family homes (made possible by the electrical grid and home oil heat), which he created from scratch in Long Island's potato fields and other such locales.[2] The movement from many families living in one big apartment block—the quintessential urban residence of the industrial era—shifts to the one-family, one-home relationship. (Today, one family—at the upper end of the income distribution—may own more than one home, thereby inverting the nineteenth-century relationship.)

One company profited from, and embodied, this newfound consumer demand and concomitant wealth generation more than any other: General Motors. The famous misquote of the time, "What's good for General Motors is good for the country," captured the solution to the paradoxes of coal capitalism that Marx had pointed to three quarters of a century earlier. (Charlie "Engine" Wilson, who left General Motors to become Eisenhower's defense secretary, actually said the converse: What was good for the nation was good for General Motors.)[3]

As David Halberstam wrote in *The Fifties*, "the only thing standing between the corporation [GM] and virtually limitless profits was the possibility of labor unrest."[4] So, after a bitter and costly strike during 1945 and 1946, executives at the car company decided that a better strategy was to buy off the United Auto Workers (UAW). The result was the so-called Treaty of Detroit, which did not merely guarantee workers traditional annual pay raises, but promised those on top COLAs (cost-of-living adjustments) tied to inflation and other factors. Here was a form of security that private sector workers had never seen in all of economic history. Other, supplemental agreements secured generous, *guaranteed* retirement benefits, including full health care and a pension that approached actual working wages. It cost GM a billion dollars; but at the time at least, it appeared to be a bargain—especially since the company could push the costs onto the consumers, who were lining up to buy the bigger and bigger car models issued each year.

What's more, GM executives knew they had wiggle room since their competitors—Ford, Chrysler, and the American Motor Company (AMC)—would have to follow suit. In fact, this was the United Auto Workers' explicit strategy: Wrest a raise or some other concession from one of the "Big Three," and the others would need to follow. The specific terms varied slightly. General Motors offered the best health benefits. AMC, by contrast, offered profit sharing to its employees. Tying wages (and pension benefits) to inflation, productivity, and especially profits would seem to solve Marx's paradox of overproduction with the swoop of a pen.

And, at least for a while, the new cooperative environment between labor and management functioned splendidly. With unionization rates high during the 1950s, marginal tax rates approaching 90 percent at the very top, the incentive structure was for everyone to do well. (U.S. unionization rates peaked in 1954, at 28 percent; today, they stand at around 11 percent.)[5] Perhaps wages were artificially capped at the top, but as long as everyone's income was growing, who minded? Not the average American. William Levitt cashed in on this new prosperity by selling the American dream to these well-paid working Americans: With almost no money down, factory workers could purchase the suburban home of their dreams. This transformation of many families from renters to owners was, of course, made possible by the automobile, which allowed employees to commute to work more easily than before. The democratization of homeownership further blunted class antagonisms by giving working Americans a stake in not only their company's financial future but the economy as a whole. (Marx had pretty much dismissed homeownership since homes were not productive capital, and they tied workers, he thought, to a locality, thereby weakening their bargaining position with employers.)

As long as demand for housing continued apace, then everyone's housing values increased (or more specifically, those in white neighborhoods—but that's another story).[6] Today, housing wealth represents over one third of all net worth for American households, and that figure is much higher for low- and moderate-income families.[7] Likewise, construction jobs were created. In 2008, the home-building industry directly employed 7.5 million workers, up from 1.25 million in 1945.[8] Welcome to the Ponzi scheme we call the American real estate market.

But this all worked because it was a relatively closed system. Who was footing the bill for high wages for American workers? American consumers, that's who. It was no big problem, since these were the same folks as the workers who were demanding and receiving higher wages—after they clocked out. Wealth, in other words, was shared fairly broadly. Hence the rosy, if overly simplistic, picture of William H. Whyte's *Organization Man*, who had time for nightly cocktails and weekend spectator sports, and his lovely wife who spent her time in coffee-chat with neighbors (what he called *kaffeeklatch*). Rising productivity and wages combined with automation led to concerns about too much spare time. What were Americans going to do with all their leisure? Such were the now risible worries of such luminary thinkers as John Kenneth Galbraith, voiced in his best seller *The Affluent Society*.

Alas, the dream couldn't last. It would collapse under the weight of its own contradictions—all the time laying the groundwork for today's economy that would replace it.

Before long, the consumer side of the American individual did what any good capitalist would do: He looked for bargains. And since the European and Japanese economies had recovered, they now offered some pretty good deals. What's more, those German and Japanese companies enjoyed technological advantages because most of their factories had to be rebuilt from scratch after the bombing campaigns of World War II had laid their predecessors to waste. So, while Pittsburgh was working with steelmaking techniques of the early 1900s, the Japanese were making the same grade metal with much more modern and economically efficient processes—not to mention starkly lower labor costs. International competition drove Detroit's (and Cleveland's and Pittsburgh's) profits into the cellar.

Why didn't we just remain a closed system and live happily ever after? you ask. Well, for one, remember this was the Oil Century, and we couldn't live on our own oil forever. In fact, we now need to import about half of all the oil we consume—a figure that will only continue to rise.[9] Even without the dependence on foreign oil, at some point these affluent Americans would have demanded access to a wide range of products from the far reaches of the globe. At some point—sooner or later—fortress America would crumble and the plastic toys would flood in. First from Japan; then from Taiwan and South Korea. And finally, from China and Southeast Asia.

If it weren't for death by a thousand imports, the Treaty of Detroit would have rotted from within, since—devoid of real competition—the system would have devolved into a Soviet-like goldbricking system of low-productivity work. Wages and prices would feed into the vicious circle of inflation, or rather stagflation (which, in fact, sparked by the oil shock of 1973, did befall us). Those generous provisions for health care and retirement have meant that American car companies (and other manufacturers) had little fat they could trim. Rather than give up defined benefit (i.e., guaranteed) pensions and health insurance for retirees, autoworkers clung to their hard-won gains—in part because union leaders are almost always closer to retirement than the rank-and-file workers they are meant to represent. In response, car companies had no choice but to move production sites overseas, slashing jobs at home in the process. Today, most of the labor that went into your patriotic Ford or Buick took place overseas. I am picking on cars to illustrate the point, but the story is no different in the rest of the manufacturing sector. The auto industry, if anything, has been spared the worst of it since there is somehow symbolic importance to "buying American" (whatever that means) to many U.S. citizens, especially veterans and politicians.

The point is: Don't blame the Asians; our midcentury system of wage growth and relative equality was going to collapse one way or another. The oil shock of 1973—when the members of OPEC took the position that they would no longer ship oil to nations that supported Israel in the Yom Kippur War, curtailing production and thereby raising prices—makes as good a marker as any for the beginning of the end. Urban manufacturing declined just as our borders were opening up. Thanks to the Hart-Cellar Act of 1965, which abolished national quotas in favor of a more flexible family reunification approach to admission, new immigrants began pouring into U.S. cities and suburbs. Low- and semi-skilled American workers were facing increased competition not only abroad but at home as well.

Meanwhile, Levittown and its heirs continued to expand, raising homeownership rates for whites who qualified for mortgages. Banks still typically "redlined" urban black neighborhoods, thereby preventing any loans from going there. During the 1970s, suburbanization continued apace, spurred by a series of court decisions ordering the racial integration of schools through busing. In other words, rather than face the prospect of either accepting black students into their children's classes or, worse still, having their own kids bused off to darker schools, whites left the cities in droves, further driving the suburban housing market. The rate of out-migration from cities was so great that in 1970, the United States became the first country in the world where a majority of the population lived in suburbs.[10] It wasn't that Americans were merely moving from downtown Cleveland to Shaker Heights. They were also moving from the Rust Belt to the Sun Belt. This, too, was a story of oil and its associated technologies. More specifically, it was a tale of air-conditioning.

Ever since the Florida doctor John Gorrie in 1851 developed a system that forced air over ice to cool the surrounding area, Americans—and particularly Southerners—would have given their right arm to have something called air-conditioning. The first chemical air conditioners relied on toxic ammonia. It wasn't until 1922 that ammonia was replaced by a more benign substance. (Toxicity didn't stop millionaire Charles Gates from building the first air-conditioned home in 1914, in normally chilly Minneapolis, no less.) By the 1920s, many movie theaters had central cooling, so that escaping summer heat was as good a reason as any to pass a couple hours in a dark room—regardless of the quality of the film being shown. Hospitals, offices, department stores, and the U.S. Congress were next to get central AC. Then, shortly after World War II, the window unit was invented. "The first window units appeared right after the war, and sales took off immediately, jumping from 74,000 in 1948 to 1,045,000 in 1958," writes Malcolm Jones, Jr. "The dripping box jutting out of the bedroom window joined the TV aerial on the roof as instant fixtures in the American suburban landscape."[11]

Partly as a result of artificial cooling, the 1960s became the first decade since the Civil War during which more Americans moved to the South than left it. In the 1970s, that trend would strengthen to the point that twice as many folks moved to Dixie than quit it. As Jones says, "Walk down the street of a Southern or Southwestern city at night, and there's no one out. All you can hear is the sound of the heat pump on the side of the house; all you can see is the blue glow behind the living-room curtains."[12] Gone were seersucker suits. Southern fashion looked not much different from what was worn in Pennsylvania or Illinois. Sunbelt cities—if you could actually call them cities—were thriving; but they were so low density, sprawling and absent any economic center, that they were really more like suburbs connected by freeway arterioles. This air-conditioned-induced mass migration would have enormous consequences for national politics as the South regained the dominant position in federal electoral politics that had been wrested away by FDR's New Deal coalition. Nixon's "Southern strategy" to peel Democrats off what was once the "solid South" could not have been better timed.

Over time, however, the commutes from the Sunbelt (and Northern) suburbs got longer, the traffic got worse, and the quality of life deteriorated. "Roughly one out of every six American workers commutes more than forty-five minutes, each way. People travel between counties the way they used to travel between neighborhoods," Nick Paumgarten noted in April 2007 in *The New Yorker.* "The number of commuters who travel ninety minutes or more each way—known to the Census Bureau as 'extreme commuters'—has reached 3.5 million, almost double the number in 1990. They're the fastest-growing category, the vanguard in a land of stagnant wages, low interest rates, and ever-radiating sprawl. They're the talk-radio listeners, billboard glimpsers, gas guzzlers, and swing voters, and they don't—can't—watch the evening news."[13] Paumgarten tells us of one man who won the Midas muffler–sponsored "longest commute" award for his round-trip daily total of 372 miles (seven hours) to Cisco Systems in San Jose, California. A fifty-seven-year-old legal secretary who works in New York gets up at four-thirty each morning in the Commonwealth of Pennsylvania. Over-all, the average commuting time is about twenty-six minutes, according to the U.S. Census Bureau—up by 18 percent since 1980.[14] No wonder we like our big, comfy SUVs in the Else-where Society.

Homeownership went hand-in-hand with suburbanization to the extent that today in the United States, two thirds of Ameri-can families live in a home they own. That figure is up from a low of 44 percent in 1940.[15] The importance of this transforma-tion of the United States from a land where a majority of citi-zens rented to one in which a veto-proof majority own their home cannot be overstated. Onetime Senate majority leader and presidential candidate Bob Dole famously remarked that he is in favor of any policy that promotes homeownership since, he claimed, homeowners vote Republican. Many folks credit the conservative revival since the 1960s to backlash against progres-sive social policies. Perhaps; but another factor—along with air-conditioning and the erosion of the solid South—is the rise of homeownership. In fact, housing tenure (whether an individual owns or rents) is one of the most important predictors of voting preference. Even at a national level, this relationship holds. If you live in a home you own—especially if you enjoy the secu-rity of owning it outright—you have less need for the govern-ment to take care of you with a strong social insurance and pension system.[16] Rather, you are actually living in your own private piggybank.

What's more, it is the family home, more than the stock mar-ket, that keeps our inequality Ponzi scheme going and that drives government policy and private choices. The median size of new homes has increased to 2,500 square feet today, up by almost 50 percent since 1976. Likewise, the proportion of new homes with four or more bedrooms has doubled and the number with three or more bathrooms has tripled in just the last twenty years. These figures, and the debt burden that drives them, make the home mortgage interest deduction the most sacrosanct federal policy after social security.[17] As a result, cheap and easy credit has been a major reason why the United States recently dipped into negative savings for the first time since the Great Depression.[18] And though manufacturing of machinery and other durable goods has pretty much flown the coop (that's the coop, not the co-op), new homes and renovations are about the only thing left that we actually physically construct ourselves. Over the last few years, housing has been responsible for just under one sixth of our GDP.[19]

The particular story of the rise in *urban* homeownership has an important sidebar: When they weren't existing rental units or SROs, many of the co-op or condo conversions were formerly office or industrial spaces—a.k.a lofts. Loft living (and working) started as an obscure practice of bohemian artists. Artists said they liked occupying large post-industrial spaces since they really couldn't afford to maintain separate homes and studios. Besides, the large windows that these former factory floors enjoyed let in lots of natural light, and the open spaces combined with high ceilings to give them room for painting, sculpture, dance, theater, and so on—space they wouldn't find in either a traditional apartment or an office-type setting.

Artists in New York, in fact, threatened to strike on September 11, 1961, if they did not get concessions from the Fire Department and other city agencies charged with enforcing building codes. (The city's population, I am sure, trembled at the prospect of its artists going on strike.) They were trapped between business and residential rules. On the one hand, commercial building codes told them they could not stay over or work odd hours in their loft studios; such regulations were meant to protect workers in the sweatshops and other factories, most of which had long since been vacated. On the other hand, residential rules forbade them, officially, from plying their trade at home. The artists of 1961, working in illegal lofts, felt like they were in hiding from building inspectors and anyone who might report them to such authorities. They decried it as a municipal shame on a city that purported to be the capital of art and culture in the Western Hemisphere.

The strike never materialized, but the artists won their battle anyway. By the end of the 1970s, "loft conversions" outpaced new housing construction in New York.[20] And of course today, the marriage of art and commerce is seen as the lifeblood of urban economic revitalization. At least since Richard Florida published *The Rise of the Creative Class* to describe the emergence of a new, powerful group of intellectual workers, ICE— as in intellectuals, culture, and education, a term coined by John Sexton, the president of New York University, to promote the university's role in the city—is seen by developers and urban planners as a necessary complement to FIRE—finance, insurance, and real estate—in any thriving, post-industrial metropolitan economy.

The lifestyle changes wrought by these artists populating former sweatshops would be so wide-reaching as to presage fundamental aspects of how many of us live our lives today. Not only has cultural production become a leading sector of the economy, but the very way that artists plied their trade back in 1961 was eerily prescient of how we all mix work and home today.[21]

By 1969, this home-work movement was really starting to gain steam. Leon Henry, who had recently completed college and decided to ignore the advice given in *The Graduate* ("Plastics, son, plastics"), recognized the trend and published a book titled *The Home Office Guide*. (Earlier, any media references to the "home office" probably meant the ministry in the United Kingdom dedicated to internal affairs.) The response was so positive that he started a monthly newsletter, *The Home Office Report*. By the time the *New York Times* bestowed its legitimacy on the subject a decade later, the number of home office workers was estimated at 5 million: larger than the dwindling number of farmers (that *other* class of home workers).

That first *Times* article, published in 1979, described a curious new breed of folks who worked from their homes. "Tucked away discreetly in corners of living rooms, behind bedroom doors, in basements, attics, garages and even bureau drawers, home offices have become the primary place of work for thousands . . ." wrote Deborah Blumenthal for the journal of record.[22] It wasn't until the following decade that the term "live-work" came into usage: "A lot of people think it is a little slice of heaven if they can live and work in their own building, so the term 'live-work situation' is appearing in ads for properties, yet some of these are illegal and prospective buyers should be on guard," R. Whittier Foote, a real estate broker, warned readers of the *New York Times* in 1987.[23] Of course, working out of one's home (which, hopefully, one owned) was nothing new, but rather a return to the past—the precapitalist past, when cottage industries were the dominant form of production.

The fact of the matter was that the type of work you could do at home was fairly limited back in 1969, 1979, or even 1987. Writers and journalists could always work from home (my mother's first "office" was a closet in our very unloftlike apartment). Artists could work from home, of course, provided there was enough space. Therapists could see patients in a room off their foyer, perhaps. An accountant might dare to receive clients in his dining room. The story of a longtime buyer for Lord &

Taylor who, after thirty-six years, started her own mail-order fashion business led to a page 1 *New York Times* article about this strange new breed of folks who combined commerce with the coziness of home.[24]

Among the benefits of such an arrangement listed by the article were savings on not having to maintain office space, not being interrupted by co-worker chitchat, flexible hours (which, we shall see, would increasingly turn from a blessing to a curse), and even being able to deduct expenses that would otherwise be considered consumption. The negatives listed back in 1979 were probably no different from those experienced by millions today: a lack of separation between professional and private lives; embarrassment when entertaining clients; a lack of face-to-face interaction with colleagues; legal problems with zoning; a dogging sense that work can be done at all hours. Sound familiar? Of course, today it's even worse since the intraviduals who belong to the Elsewhere class are working all the time. Furthermore, it doesn't really matter whether you intended to have a home office or not: If you work in the so-called creative class, you've got one in your hand—it's called an iPhone, a Black-Berry, or a Treo. About the only thing that has eased since 1979 is the social stigma of working from home. After all, if work is everywhere now, what's the big deal?

As in the case of the zoning rules that made live-work lofts illegal, the tax system initially fought the home office trend. One case involved a schoolteacher who was not allowed to do her curricular work in the classroom thanks to safety and contract concerns. Instead, she prepared her classes in her tiny apartment and claimed part of her apartment costs as a business expense. The IRS disallowed two thirds of her home office deduction, but the U.S. Tax Court overturned the ruling, giving her the full amount she claimed. Another especially ironic story involved a lawyer for the IRS itself who claimed a home office deduction since he did professional reading and research during off-hours in a study at his place of residence. Though the IRS headquarters was not far away and was, in fact, open around the clock, he claimed that it was more pleasant to work from home, and in turn, that $100 of his annual $2,100 rent was a professional business expense. His boss, the IRS commissioner, overruled him, but the U.S. Tax Court found in his favor; his victory was short-lived, however, as a Court of Appeals ruled against him.[25]

The IRS understandably fought this growing trend, but the results coming out of the courts were ambiguous. Clearly, the government didn't know how to deal with this new phenomenon. In an effort to achieve some fiscal clarity, the 1976 Tax Reform Act severely narrowed the definition of the home office for tax purposes. The 1986 Tax Reform Bill took another stab. To take a deduction for a part of your home that you used for income-generating purposes, you now had to meet two main criteria: (1) You had to show that you used the home office regularly. The best way to show this was to have no other place of business for that activity—that is, you generally can't have a separate office for your writing, away from home, and then also take the home office deduction. (2) It couldn't be used for other purposes.[26] You couldn't, in other words, work there five days a week and then serve cocktails to your guests on Saturday night. You couldn't even manage your investment portfolio there. But you could see patients or clients there. Of course, today with so much crossover between socializing and work, and between investment and consumption, how's the IRS (or you, for that matter) going to know the difference?

Such confusion was already apparent in a case that worked its way through the courts during the early 1990s: *Soliman* v.

Internal Revenue Service. Dr. Nader Soliman was an anesthesiologist who was affiliated with three hospitals but who had no office in any of them. To manage his practice, he converted his third bedroom into an office complete with filing cabinets for patient records, copier, desk, and so on. He spent an average of two hours per day there keeping the books, checking in with surgeons, preparing presentations, and reading medical journals. The IRS had ruled that since his principal income-generating activity was putting patients to sleep, and since he did that elsewhere, he was not allowed to claim the deduction. First the Tax Court and then the Federal Appeals Court ruled 2–to–1 in his favor, throwing out the "focal point" test—meaning the home office no longer had to be the exclusive or even the principal site of the income-generating activity. The Court of Appeals instructed the IRS to use instead a "facts and circumstances" test, paving the way for salespeople, for example, to claim the deduction even though most of their time is spent on the road. The IRS dragged its feet, refusing to apply *Soliman* to other scenarios; its foot-dragging paid off, for in 1993, the U.S. Supreme Court reversed the lower courts with an 8–to–1 decision that established that the home office needed to be the principal place of business.[27]

I mentioned that back thirty years ago there wasn't much that could be done at home in terms of work. That's not quite true: You could have worked the land. In fact, between 1960 and 1980, the total number of Americans working at home declined substantially. This reflected, actually, the final death of the family farm in America. (In 1900, 38 percent of the U.S. population lived and worked on farms. By 2000, that figure stood at 2 percent.)[28] From 1980 onward, however, the figure rebounded, rising by 56 percent during the 1980s, and by another 23 percent in the 1990s. This new breed of home workers were more highly educated than their officebound counterparts (34 percent more likely to have a graduate degree, for instance). And almost half of them were salary or wage employees—up from a third in 1980. In other words, folks were actually working traditional jobs from their bedrooms! And these stats are using the strict definition of the U.S. Census for the primary place of work. If we use a broader definition of using your home as an office regularly but not exclusively, then almost one third of U.S. workers did so as recently as 2004.[29] If these trends continue, don't be surprised if another Supreme Court challenge surfaces—especially given the antitax leanings of the current Court makeup.

Of course, the thing—and I do mean thing—that came along to change the possibilities of home work was the personal computer and its associated "revolution." And, of course, that, too, had its roots in the 1950s—at least if we consider the fifties as having really started in the postwar 1940s. On Valentine's Day, 1946, a University of Pennsylvania research team completed ENIAC, the first electronic computer, weighing in at almost 30 tons. Other computers had many of its capabilities, but what made it unique at the time was its reprogrammability to a full range of computational tasks (i.e., it was not dedicated to a single function). This adaptability required over 17,000 vacuum tubes, 70,000 resistors, over 7,000 diodes, and thousands of other components, all held together by over 5 million hand-soldered connections.* Fast-forward thirty years to the arrival of the personal computer. The Apple II had appeared in 1977, along with others such as the PET 2001; by 1979 already, there were half a million personal computers being sold.[30]

Long before the advent of personal computing and the so-

---

*Its main purpose at the time? Helping to build the hydrogen bomb—only the single most destructive invention in human history still to this day.

called information age, scientists worried about the impact computers would have on human society. A fourteen-page memorandum sent by leading scientists to President Lyndon B. Johnson declared that computerization was likely to create massive unemployment. "Cybernation," which the authors argued resulted from "the combination of the computer and the automated self-regulating machine," was "already reorganizing the economic and social system to meet its own needs"—in 1964, no less. Others, who put a more optimistic spin on the work-saving impact of automation (and later computers), worried about what Americans would do with all their new leisure time. John Maynard Keynes famously fretted in a 1930 essay, "Economic Possibilities for Our Grandchildren," over how humans would spend their time in a meaningful way when work was no longer necessary.

And it was true—at least at first: Over the course of the 1950s and 1960s, average work hours decreased as Americans became more productive and the economy grew at a good clip. But, as history actually played out, these worries about how to fill the hours of the day with something more important than spectator sports, bridge, bingo, or backgammon were a tad premature. First, it turns out that we spend slightly more time doing unpaid labor (housework and the like) than we did even in 1900. Second, much of the other time we aren't formally working we are spending in school.[31] What's more, after declining for most of the century, the proportion of American men who worked more than fifty hours per week started to increase around 1970—especially among the highest-paid, salaried men.[32] As for women, the higher their own household incomes, the more they perceive a time crunch even with the same paid and unpaid work hours as their lower-income counterparts.[33] It is this frenetic feeling that time is money, which evinces the craziness that many professionals feel. It is the shadow cost of not working more that drives dissatisfaction. This is a key point: It is the plethora of economic opportunities created by technology that creates a dogging sense of loss, of needing to be elsewhere, doing something different. It is the fact that we make more money now than ever before (among the top half) that creates those unfinished lists of tasks in our heads. The more we make, the more economic opportunities we "enjoy," the more we are haunted in the Elsewhere economy.

We used to bitterly resist additional work requirements—to the point of bloody union strikes. Today, only one in ten workers belongs to a union and nobody has to coerce us to keep on working. And this inculcation of Benjamin Franklin's work–ethic–gone–mad is not just a story of long hours; despite recent talk that job tenure has irreversibly decreased, the fact is that most of us stick with the same employer for most of our working lives. The average length of our longest time span at any one employer has declined only slightly, from 21.9 years for those approaching retirement age (58 to 62 years old) in 1969 to 21.4 years for those in the same age bracket in 2002.[34] It certainly remains possible that among the youngest cohort of workers this figure will have drastically declined; but that remains to be determined. It may not be that we are changing jobs as often as the media seems to imply; perhaps it's just the feeling of an ax hanging over our heads as we toil at our desks that propels us to work superlong weeks. In fact, many Americans love their work so much that they do it for free. The newest form of production—known alternatively as open-source or commons-based production—involves huge numbers of folks working on divisible tasks for no compensation. The most prominent examples of this Communist-like system are, perhaps, Wiki-pedia and LINUX. Many proponents of open-source production models champion this approach as an alternative to traditional capitalism.

On the other hand, one can see this as the ultimate triumph of big business. Take the ESP game that matches random individuals online and then asks them to enter words that describe a photo they are each shown. They "win" when they enter descriptors of the image that match. Sounds like fun? Actually, it's work. Players are tagging images for Google's database. The rationale is that when two strangers converge upon the same label, that label must be a pretty decent representation of the photo. But, of course, when Google actually asks folks to do this work *explicitly* through a volunteer Web site, hardly anybody does. Or take computer scientist Louis von Ahn's Recaptcha Project. Captchas are those wavy words you enter at the end of online transactions to make sure you are a person and not a computer bot. The Recaptcha Project adds a second wavy word to participating websites. These words are not known to the computer but rather are excerpted from scans of old manuscripts and periodicals as part of efforts to digitize the universe. When the optical text recognition software stumbles upon a word—due to the poor quality of the original or a unique font—the text is farmed out to you, the user, to decipher. That is, when you enter two Captchas on a Web site, only one constitutes the actual test of your personhood. The other is work that you are doing for the *New York Times*, Google, and Louis. Work and leisure have collapsed.

Or maybe we just want to escape the chaos of home life, as some sociologists have suggested, and find work to be a calming refuge from family demands (home offices, of course, threw a wrench into that plan).[35] After all, solving a software problem for our employer (or for our open-source community) may feel a lot more rewarding than taking out the garbage, doing the shopping, or scrubbing the oven. Whatever the reasons for our longer hours, the result is a blurring of the line between work and leisure. Does debugging Firefox count as work or leisure? Since we are not being paid for it and it's not housework, it probably falls into the leisure category. (Although some economists argue that programmers, in particular, use open-source work to signal their skills to potential employers.) And if we are on a fixed salary and take on extra work to "get ahead," is that work? Or is it just another dressed-up form of leisure? Or what about updating our garage band's MySpace site at 2:00 a.m.? After all, it is for our band, which we hope will be discovered in the not-too-distant future. That's an investment, isn't it?

For most of the industrial era, machines were used to augment or replace humans in performing *some* physical tasks. Now, with computerization, they were replacing *some* mental tasks as well. The economists Frank Levy and Richard Murnane put the emphasis on *some* since, they point out, a robot could not change a baby's diaper. Similarly, computers (so far) are not very good at synthesizing data to see patterns on their own. They have no interpretive ability. Thus computers, according to Levy and Murnane, create as many jobs as they eliminate. They do this by stimulating economic growth by lowering costs for the tasks they do well: Computers "shift work away from routine tasks and towards . . . expert thinking and complex communication." The jobs they tend to displace don't involve much independent thought, but rather raw computational or processing ability. They get rid of these low-skilled jobs in two ways: (1) by doing them themselves (e.g., through voice recognition phone trees); and (2) by allowing others in lower-wage labor markets to do them for us (as in the much maligned and much celebrated call centers in India).

The result is that the jobs created over the last forty years have not gotten more specific; they have actually gotten broader.[36] With computerization, we are not, on average, rendered into mindless number punchers. Rather, computers have taken over many rote tasks, and instead, we need to be able to synthesize, process, and draw abstractions from the increasing amounts of data that are presented to us. Gone is the secretary whose principal role is to take dictation, answer the phone, and type up memos. Enter the administrative assistant, who may need to know how to edit Web pages in HTML, manage Google Calendar for the entire office, book travel arrangements (a task once handled by a professional class of travel agents), and so on.

This broadening of job roles contributes to our anxiety as well. That is, we also may feel as if we've never completely learned our job. In other words, the auto line worker of Henry Ford's Tayloristic plant could be secure in knowing that the rules and expectations of his task were transparent and relatively simple (perhaps mind-numbingly so). Ditto for the coal miner of the nineteenth century and the farmer of the eighteenth. Yes, there was always pressure to keep up the speed and keep down the error rate, but contrast that with today's knowledge worker, who needs to be able to multitask, constantly learn new computer programs, and generally adapt to a fluid work flow of highly variable tasks. It's not that our jobs have necessarily gotten harder, but the increase in variance in our everyday tasks and the fact that they require more mental concentration and cognitive skills may be quite stress-inducing. There is always a new surprise just around the corner for the knowledge worker.

The boring jobs that can be delegated to computers have been. Others that can't have been outsourced to low-wage labor markets (the famous Indian call centers), thanks to telecommunications technologies. The only low-skilled jobs that really remain in the United States are those which involve personal contact that cannot be performed from afar. It's no surprise that the fastest-growing low-wage occupations are food service prepara-tion, followed by home health care workers.[37] After all, you can't very well get a computer or a call service center to wipe your incontinent grandmother or serve her three hot meals a day.

The result—most economists agree—is an increasing skill and education premium. In 1979, Levy and Murnane write, the difference in median wages between a thirty-year-old col-lege graduate and a high school graduate of the same age stood at 17 percent. A mere twenty-one years later, that differ-ence had ballooned to 50 percent. Now computers, certainly, were not the only cause of that difference (nor was globaliza-tion), but there is little doubt that they played a prominent role in widening the income gap over the last thirty years. And those median levels are just the proverbial tip of the iceberg. Computers and telecommunications technologies have allowed for private equity managers to make tens of millions of dol-lars through international arbitrage while sitting in their paja-mas in Westport, Connecticut (also known as "Northern Hedg-istan" to financial industry insiders). As much as the left likes to blame Ronald Reagan (and the two Bushes) for the steady rise in income inequality, much of it had to do with computer technology.

And then there are the second-order effects of rising inequal-ity on the economy. Paradoxically, the fastest-growing number of jobs in the first decade of the third millennium is projected to be in food preparation and service.[38] Computers were supposed to eliminate low-skilled jobs and create high-skilled ones. So, what's happening here? It's an indirect effect: the inequality itself creates the low-wage serving jobs. After all, the high-wage workers are—for the first time in history—working more hours than their lower-wage counterparts. In other words, the substitution effect (greater opportunity costs of not working) is swamping the income effect (greater ability to afford not to work). These high-wage families don't have time to prepare home-cooked meals. Home life can be and is being outsourced. Hence the rise of low-wage food prep and serving: Welcome to the new Feudalism, twenty-first-century style.

Part of the story of the growth of the food services industry is, of course, the entry of women into the labor market. Today, almost two thirds of women with children under six years of age work (63 percent); by contrast, the figure was just over one third (39 percent) in 1975.[39] Instead of cooking for their families, many low-wage women now reheat preprocessed food for other families in the restaurant industry. Instead of waiting on their own husband and kids, many women without college degrees wait on *your* kids. (Waitressing is, in fact, the number one profession for women without a college education.)[40]

This story of women's rising labor force participation has the potential to increase economic inequality when it combines with what demographers call *assortative mating*—otherwise known as like-marrying-like. That is, since 1967, the demographer Christine Schwartz demonstrates that among two-earner couples, the similarity in their wages has risen by about threefold. In other words, whereas women used to look for good earners to marry, now men do so, too. What's more, in the 1960s, when a husband earned more money, it usually meant that his wife didn't have to work (or was less likely to). But today, when a man earns more money, it means that his wife is probably earning more money, too. In 1967, Schwartz reports, when a man was at the bottom of the income hierarchy, the chances that his wife earned at least some money that year were about 65 percent; the wife of a man in the top 10 percent of earners, by contrast, had less than a 40 percent chance of having earned some cash in that year.

By 2003, the curve was essentially flat. In total, the changing nature of marriage probably explains about 40 percent of the rise in income inequality.[41] And that's not counting the fact that higher-income folks are more likely to be married in the first place.

There is potentially a forward-feeding cycle here. As inequality rises, couples are no longer content to rely on one income, or even one "main" earner combined with a part-time secondary worker's wages. No, increasingly many families feel they need two full-time workers in the labor force to "keep up." This may even drive men (and women) to increasingly select women (and men) for their earning potential over other noneconomic characteristics. These dynamics, in turn, fuel rising inequality, and the whole cycle begins again. The end result is, of course, continuously rising inequality, the outsourcing of previously nonmarket processes (like cooking dinner), ever-escalating work hours, and the development of technologies to facilitate constant labor. Welcome to Elsewhere, U.S.A.

What's also important to note is that with the entry of women into the labor force as breadwinners, what were once the personal choices in our intimate lives—decisions about sex, love, and reproduction—have become matters of economic concern. While women always faced the risk of marrying an economic dud, now men face that possibility as well. Meanwhile, women face stark economic choices in deciding when—and if—to have children, what career track to take, and so on, as they try to balance work and family. (And an increasing number of men who play a significant role in child rearing also face these conundrums.) The family home—meaning the house itself—is no longer a private sphere, set apart from economic profit making. Now, with two thirds of Americans owning the home in which they live, domestic life right down to the choice of neighbors and drapery involves economic calculations. So much for relaxing at the family hearth. As you sip your cocoa in front of the wood-burning fireplace, you better consider refinancing before interest rates get worse.

WHERE WE ARE AT

So, we have gone from a country with high ceilings and fans to low ceilings and air-conditioning; we have gone from an economy where many workers serviced one machine to one in which each American has dozens of machines working for them over the course of a given day; we have gone from being a nation of wandering renters to ever more rooted homeowners; we have gone from a country that experienced race riots in the 1960s—during a period of economic growth spread relatively equally across income deciles—to a country of almost Third World levels of economic inequality, where solid majorities vote to repeal the estate tax. We used to enjoy our free time and left the Europeans to work more than us; now we have more kids to take care of than they do, even as we work significantly more hours.*

No one single factor—not air-conditioning or computers; not female labor force participation; not tax policy alone or immigration—has caused these dramatic shifts. In fact, it is probably a futile exercise to ask how much tax policy drove the develop-

---

*Americans work an average of 25.1 hours per week (averaged across all working-age persons) in contrast to Germans, for instance, who average 18.6 hours. We work over 6 more weeks than the French per year. See Alberto Alessina, Edward L. Glaeser, and Bruce Sacerdote, "Work and Leisure in the U.S. and Europe: Why So Different?" Working Paper no. 11278, National Bureau of Economic Research, Cambridge, Mass., 2005.

ment of computers, how much computers drive income inequality, and how much income inequality drives commuting distances. Better to take a deep breath and unfocus the eyes to try to take in the entire mosaic that makes up the social landscape today.

If our new economy was indeed born out of the paradoxes of the last one, then the technological seeds were planted—ironically—back in the halcyon days of the 1950s. I say "ironically" since it is the idealized version of the fifties that forms the backdrop against which we measure the so-called inadequacies of today. Ah, what a time. Liberals pine for those days when income inequality was at its lowest point of the century and the top marginal tax rates exceeded the now unimaginable level of 90 percent.[42] And that with a Republican in the White House. Meanwhile, conservatives pine for the family structure of that epoch—as in *Leave It to Beaver, Father Knows Best,* or a number of other shows that purported to reflect the nuclear family in 1950s U.S. households via the cathode ray tube in their living room. In fact, never have women stayed at home to such a degree.[43] Perhaps the irony we should take away is that high marginal tax rates and low levels of inequality equal "traditional" nuclear families with stay-at-home moms and low divorce rates. Or perhaps it's just a coincidence.

Today, the UAW has more members who are retirees than are workers. That creates a strange set of incentives as they move toward negotiations with employers who have traditionally guaranteed generous (defined benefit) pensions and retiree health care coverage. The best estimate is that retirement health care burdens translate to an additional cost of $1,000 per vehicle for GM. In fact, a prominent government economist once described General Motors to me as a pension and health insurance provider that sells cars to finance itself. Meanwhile, in order to survive in the post-industrial economy, the UAW has expanded beyond the traditional automotive industry not just to other manufacturing sectors but also to service workers. In line with its identity as representing skilled workers, the UAW doesn't generally include burger flippers but rather "intellectual workers," technical workers like engineers, clerical employees like government bureaucrats, as well as journalists, graduate students, and even 5,000 members of the National Writers Union.[44]

A curious aspect of economic succession that had been noted by Marx and others was that the new ruling class for a given economic transformation tended to emerge out of the margins of the existing social order. For example, while nobody should shed any tears for the old feudal aristocracy, who did just fine during the modern industrial epoch, they did not form the essential core of the capitalist class. Rather, the newly powerful bourgeoisie emerged from the often landless trading and merchant class, which rose to power as technological development and urbanization proceeded. Similarly, in Communist countries, it was the intellectuals who took over the state bureaucracy who flourished.[45] Those American artists who "hid out" during the late 1950s and early 1960s in illegal lofts gave birth to the newly powerful creative class of the new millennium. While individual artists themselves probably attained or retained little power (though, had they purchased their loft conversions, they would have made millions), they spawned a whole new economy. Not only do places like Richmond, Virginia, and even Princeton, New Jersey, now brag that they offer "downtown lofts" (even if some of these are, in fact, new constructions made to look like old industrial conversions), a bohemian-type lifestyle has come to dominate the upper echelons of the new economy. By this I don't just mean that—as Richard Florida asserts—"creativity" is now cherished and rewarded in a growing sector of the high-wage economy. I mean that the very rhythms of work of most professionals today could be clearly seen in the natural light of the artist live-work lofts of 1960: an integration of home and work; odd hours; individualized, nonsalaried work; status insecurity; social networking; and so on. We are all artists now.

We are also all geeks now. The skinny, bespectacled kid who had the sand kicked in his face at the beach in the fifties advertisements for Charles Atlas's bodybuilding program now runs the company. With a few notable exceptions, the wealth of industrial-age captains of industry generally came from steel, railroads, automobiles. These robber barons of the Gilded Age conveyed a public image of heft—befitting their chosen sectors—as well as grumpiness. (J. P. Morgan would assault anyone who dared try to take his photo on account of suffering from the skin disease rosacea; and he claimed that he "owed the public nothing.") The nineteenth-century economist Thorstein Veblen wrote that these businessmen were akin to barbarians who gained their riches by raping and pillaging rather than by producing it themselves. When it came time for them to leave their mark, their philanthropy became associated with colossal buildings such as Rockefeller Center, the New York Public Library, and Carnegie Hall. Contrast that to the efforts of Bill Gates, Warren Buffett, and Michael Bloomberg, who have dedicated their wealth—made from "soft" industries—to addressing such issues as malaria and education. It is to this new world of work built by folks like Bloomberg and Google's Sergey Brin and Larry Page that we now turn.

One Plus a Hundred Zeros

Welcome to Your (N)Office

If there is any "center" or "downtown" to our new economy (and to Elsewhere, U.S.A., for that matter) it is just off the 101 Freeway in Mountain View, California. The headquarters of the information economy, so to speak, is Google.com, whose mission, elegantly stated, is "to organize the world's information and make it universally accessible and useful." Started as a Ph.D. research project, and incorporated in a friend's Silicon Valley garage, Google epitomizes the Elsewhere Ethic better than any other company. The very service itself could not be more representative of the networked or Elsewhere Society: the search engine deploys an algorithm that ranks Web pages' appropriateness not so much by their own content as by the number of other pages that refer ("link") to them.

Arriving at the "Googleplex," as the campus of office buildings is called, to attend a "Scifoo"—an "un-conference" science camp hosted by Google, the British scientific journal *Nature*, and the O'Reilly Media Group—I realized that I had parked on the wrong side of the complex. Not to worry. There were free bikes left at various stations. I hopped on one and found my way around to Building 40.

As I wove through the main central area, I passed a huge dinosaur skeleton (bought by Google co-founder Larry Page on eBay) posed so that it was chasing a flock of pink lawn flamingos, a huge sandbox with a volleyball net strung over it, and an herb and tomato garden growing out of plastic "Earthboxes" meant for high-density soilless agriculture in the developing world. Above the Google reception desk a liquid crystal display offered a scrolling list of searches going on across the world. It is said that Google employees can see how news breaks across the globe in real time by watching searches on, say, Britney Spears or a major earthquake, spreading across the globe like an information tsunami.

Once I found Building 40, I was no less astonished by the inside. In order to put the "camp" into the science camp, plastic sheets had been fixed to the floors, on which blow-up rafts, tents, and sleeping bags dotted the internal landscape. A huge schedule board was propped up against one wall, where some Scifoo campers were busy annotating new sessions they wanted to host while others scanned the current offerings. Almost the entire two-and-a-half-day event was unscripted. The sessions, demos, discussions, and so on were meant to emerge organically in an open-source fashion from the couple hundred participants. The casual scribbles on the schedule grid ("3-d printing"; "the future history of biology"; "the tricorder is here"; "just when you thought it was safe to teach evolution") belied the polished professional presentations to which they pertained.

As I hurried to the one I wanted to hear, I passed a piano, a pinball machine, a video arcade game, posters advertising talks to come (the Amazing Randi, the magician, would speak on Monday), refrigerators with cold drinks, snack stands, and the Building 40 cafeteria—known as Charlie's, the name of the first chef at Google who had previously been chef to The Grateful Dead. The cafeteria was one of many on campus. There is one, for example, that serves only vegan food; there is a smoothie bar located next to the gym; and there are many micro-kitchens, as they are called, dotted along the numerous byways and conference rooms. What is common to all of them is the price: nothing.

All of the food and beverages are complimentary to Googlers and their guests (hence use of the gym was also free so that employees could work off all those cookies). Free food is provided not just during business hours but on the weekends—this forms a key part of the extended work-life human resources strategy. Though it makes economic sense upon reflection, it was this costless food—more than the dinosaur in the courtyard or the lectures by magicians—that stunned me. First of all, only in a post-industrial economy would food be cheap enough for such a plan to even be considered (even if prices are beginning to rise, the impact will most acutely be felt in developing countries). In all other epochs, food was a major expense, and only farmwork ers and restaurant employees were ever provided it free of charge. (It was, in fact, one of the rationales for allowing lower than minimum wages in these two industries.)

The amenities of home don't stop with food. You can drop off your laundry and dry cleaning in boxes for valet service, or you can do your own laundry for free at the washers/dryers located in the basements of select buildings. You can socialize there, too. There are field hockey games twice a week on the campus. Sound like fun? That's the point. If it sounds a little too fun, don't worry. Any consumption-induced guilt will be assuaged by the eco-friendly atmosphere. Google's utensils are potato starch–based (though the company admits that one employee experimented with burying a fork for a year and it did not seem to biodegrade much in that period). And the company is busy installing thousands of solar panels to help make itself carbon-neutral. (Other strategies include energy-saving measures and the purchase of carbon offsets.)

The abundance of free food and toys *does* make the campus an attractive place to spend time; indeed, I lured my children to come along to the second day of Scifoo camp by assuring them they could eat as much junk as they wanted and play computer games as long as their hearts desired (a since unrepeated experiment in total freedom). I was not alone in being blown away by this alternate model of labor management: *Fortune* magazine rated the company the number one employer in 2006. Where else can you get a massage anytime you want at work (appointment required, however)? Babette, the Massage Programs Manager, tells us that there are all sorts of options, ranging from prenatal massage to "healing modalities" such as Bowen work. She jokes that folks want to work at Google just for the massages, reputed to be unparalleled on the outside world. Like a crack dealer, the company provides each N'oogler (a contraction of New Googler) a coupon for a free hour-long massage upon arrival. (Who needs an equally stressed out spouse to go home to when you've got Babette?)

As one online commenter put it: "Google is setting the bar for human-oriented corporate culture. Sure, some ideas may push beyond what seems sensible now, but you don't know until you try. Employees can now start really thinking about what they want from a company, rather than just picking what a company deemed to offer them. You go Google!"[1] Another complains that the massages aren't free all the time: "Surely if a Google employee really wants a free Googlmassage [sic] they shouldn't need a voucher in the first place?"[2]

But underneath the subsidized acupressure and the games of foozball, there are perhaps some more insidious economic calculations happening. The CEO himself, Eric Schmidt, is fairly up-front about the expected return in all this human investment: "The goal is to strip away everything that gets in our employees' way. Let's face it: programmers want to program, they don't want to do their laundry. So we make it easy for them to do both."

What he doesn't mention is that wages are lower than they are at other Silicon Valley competitors. For example, a systems administrator generally starts at $35,000 a year. Economists will knowingly nod and say that for a large company (Google has about 14,000 employees) there is no escaping the general rule that benefits (even potato chips and unlimited sodas) generally come out of wages, if not quite at a 1-to-1 ratio. Given than Silicon Valley is one of the most expensive real estate markets in the country, how does a young geek survive on $35K? Plenty of gardeners and other laborers triple up in dormitory-style rooms in poorer sections of the South Bay such as East Palo Alto. Many maids drive hours at daybreak to clean the plush houses they tend in places like Atherton, Mountain View, and Los Altos. Google, however, addresses the mismatch between wages and rents by offering a free shuttle bus service to San Francisco and the East Bay (neither of which is a dirt-cheap place to live). The catch? Well, there's the same old issue that the cost is probably coming out of wages. But the real drawback is that there is free WiFi on the bus itself.

How is this a problem? you may ask. It means that you can work during your commute. (Of course, you don't *have* to . . .) Did I mention that you can even work as you stand at the urinal or sit on the plush seat of the combined toilet/directional bidet? Taking a page—literally—from those English pubs that post sections of the newspaper above urinals for drunken pissers to read while they lean forward to relieve their bladders, Google has taken to posting little educational flyers for their coders to peruse as they relieve themselves. In episode 52 (the lessons are built around a continuous narrative), a green lightbulb declares that "Testing rocks!" and a red symbol laments that "Debugging sucks," imparting the computer programming equivalent to "A stitch in time saves nine" before launching into rather technical advice about code testing. But if you don't stop working when you're on the toilet, you might as well work everywhere. In fact, that's in Google's bullet-pointed corporate philosophy, too. Right above some other notables (#6 "You can make money without doing evil" and #9 "You can be serious without a suit"), coming in at number 5 on the Letterman-like top ten list, is: "You don't need to be at your desk to need an answer." While they are ostensibly talking about their customers, they might as well be referring to the Googlers themselves.

It should come as no surprise, then, that the company was born on the Stanford University campus rather than the symbolic garage in which it was actually incorporated. In fact, the college campus feel is the explicit aim of co-founders Larry Page and Sergey Brin. In addition to lectures by the Amazing Randi, Googlers might find on offer a technical discourse on some aspect of code sampling or a political speech by John McCain. Desks are clustered in dense packs in shared offices to mimic the arrangement of servers and to facilitate work-time chitchat (though employees are issued noise cancellation headphones on their first day of work). The sheer density of humans at the Googleplex outdoes any office setting other than, perhaps, the newsroom of a large urban newspaper. It feels like a bright, colorful knowledge sweatshop—and a college dorm.

About the only other major domain of life absent from the campus is regular on-site child care. Although there is a clearinghouse for Google employees to find quality child care and there are emergency care drop-off centers at the Googleplex itself, along with plenty of toys to occupy kids who are brought to work in a pinch, there is not yet a full-scale day care center or lab school. Perhaps this "oversight" can be attributed to the generally young, childless life stage of most of the workers there. In fact, I would not be surprised if Google soon installs dorms on or near the Googleplex, since this move would be the next logical step in the complete breakdown of the home/work distinction. (Or maybe before dorms Google might allow cats at work; currently only dogs are welcome.) In short, Google approximates a "total institution" perhaps more than any other private corporation since the days of company towns run by mining interests.

A total institution is a social environment where the participants experience all aspects of their lives—meals, sleeping, grooming, socializing, recreation, and so on. Common examples of total institutions are military barracks, prisons, mental hospitals, and university campuses. Perhaps, then, it is partly an ironic consequence of the major expansion of higher education up through the 1970s—and on-campus living in particular—that work and home life have blended so. Or perhaps it is the entry of women into the labor force rearing its head again: You can take the woman out of the kitchen, so to speak, but you can't take the kitchen out of the woman. When the primary child rearers come to the office, the office culture is going to change, just as American culture not only affects the immigrants it assimilates but is itself, in turn, altered by their incorporation.

These changes in the nature of work are not limited to business but now extend to government as well, despite its traditional reputation as a laggard in organizational innovation. One of the first governmental innovations that Mayor Mike (that is, Michael Bloomberg) brought to City Hall was reorganizing the space of City Hall itself. Like any New Yorker who renovates their newly acquired commercial or residential space, Bloomberg had the existing offices ripped out and replaced with his own design. He imported the layout he had used successfully at his news corporation, Bloomberg, LLP. In this "bullpen" style, which mimicked the system used at many a newsroom, the perimeter offices are replaced with mini-conference rooms that folks can reserve for meetings (or which can be commandeered for impromptu brainstorming sessions). When doing humdrum tasks—that is, staring at a computer screen—workers sit in cubicles in the center of the space. This even goes for Hizzoner, the mayor himself, whose cubicle is no bigger or smaller than everyone else's. Space no longer equals status. Gone are the trappings and symbolism of the corner office. To be unplugged and immersed in the flow of human and digital traffic is the new status symbol.

Whereas in the industrial epoch, the ability to cloister oneself off from the hoi polloi was a mark of power; in the post-industrial, networked economy, being surrounded by as many people as possible, all seeking your attention, is the ultimate manifestation of rank. Or, better yet, do away with the cubicles altogether: The oft-cited Pew Internet Study reports that a third of Internet users at any given time are accessing the World Wide Web from a third space—that is, a café, a library, even a public park. When we do want to make ourselves scarce, we don't wall ourselves in; we release ourselves into the world, seeking privacy in public space, while others back at the office may be left to imagine we are at important meetings to which they themselves have not been invited.

CAN WE ALL GET ALONG?

Still, even with free food, bullpen offices, and intense networking, economic relations are not all peachy-keen in contemporary America. There are social tensions and misunderstandings that result from the mix of the economic red shift, portable workshop, and price culture. That's because whereas industrial capitalism offered very distinct roles complete with impregnable boundaries, the service sector and the much celebrated "flattened" organizational structure of the new economy have destroyed them. Hence the authority confusion that has led to awkward social relations and lots of misunderstandings in the world of work (and weisure).

According to Max Weber, there are three possible bases for authority. The first is traditional—we agree to do things that our higher-ups ask of us because that's the way things have always been done. Hereditary monarchies, Islamic law, and the Jewish Torah are all examples of traditional authority. The second type of authority was labeled *charismatic* by Weber. Charismatic authority rests on the special aura of a particular individual. Picture Adolf Hitler's or Benito Mussolini's grip on their respective peoples. Or think Elvis. If the King had ever asked his fans to move a mountain, many of them would have pushed real hard. And let's not forget the cult leaders —someone like Jim Jones, who led a mass suicide in Guyana in the 1970s that sparked the phrase "Drink the Kool-Aid." All of these individuals have enjoyed charismatic authority—that *je ne sais quoi* that makes followers willing to acquiesce to their demands.

But in modern capitalism, Weber asserted, both traditional and charismatic authority were supposed to be eclipsed by *legal-rational* authority. This last type rests not in an individual person but rather in a particular social role. The instructor has authority over her students not because she's especially cool but because she holds the title of professor. The manager holds sway over factory workers because he occupies a particular position within a bureaucracy (the firm). The authority attendant to these positions comes partly from the very fact that it is separate from the individual and instead attached to the office she holds. It also stems from the fact that in the modern bureaucratic organization, even the boss herself has a boss all the way up the food chain. The buck stops nowhere, as everyone supposedly answers to some greater authority, and thus they can always appeal to that higher authority (the vice president, the board of trustees, the American voters) in order to legitimate their own request. Lastly, legal-rational authority is honored since it supposedly follows (and is constrained by) formal rules. As the governor of Massachusetts, for example, you can ask your assistant to take dictation because that is part of the job description. You cannot ask him to babysit your kids, since that is outside the formally defined bounds of his role, as Republican governor Jane Swift quickly found out when the *Boston Globe* got wind of this.

Legal-rational authority worked really well for the "Organization Man" of the 1950s, when large corporations were the center of economic life. Bureaucracy—whether military, educational, commercial, or governmental—is made for (and by) legal-rational authority. Modern capitalism, with its penetrating bureaucracy, was supposed to lead to ever-increasing depersonalization of economic relations. But as casual Fridays evolved into casual every day, and the firms of the new economy flattened out the organization chart and gave each employee stock options, the bureaucratic basis of legal-rational authority was inadvertently dissolved. Now, the distinction between role and person has broken down, and leaders can no longer appeal to the higher authorities they claim are setting the agenda.

As a result, today we can witness charismatic authority making a comeback of sorts. It is the charismatic CEO who gets the biggest stock option package. It is the visionary social entrepreneur who builds a multimillion-dollar not-for-profit from a shell of a Web site. If that were all that's afoot, it would be no big deal. But the erosion of legal-rational authority has turned much of economic relations inside out: The parent is afraid to scold the nanny, because she feels guilty about spending so much time away from her toddler. Instead, the babysitter lectures the parent when she is late coming home from a meeting. The dental hygienist tut-tuts at the rich patient for failing to floss in between cleanings. And the executive hires a personal trainer for the express purpose of inducing guilt about his poor workout habits. The aspiring actress running late for a casting call has a negative interaction with her taxi driver since she was talking on her cell phone, and didn't offer her destination quickly enough. He is rude to her. But instead of refusing to tip, she actually tips extra because he has aroused in her some half buried feeling of cultural privilege—even though their take-home pay is equal. The personal nature of these economic transactions contorts what would have been straightforward class relations in any other epoch.

When I spoke with young Google employees about this new paradigm and their experiences with it, I expected to find the same cynicism that I brought to my first job. "Yeah, the pay sucks, but you gotta do what you gotta do to pay the rent, right?" Or perhaps, "I can't stand the fact that my boss knows one tenth what I do but gets paid double." No dice: These were happy campers. I even probed with leading questions such as, "Don't you think it's ridiculous that Craig and Brin paint themselves as heroes for taking only one dollar in salary when they're worth billions in stock?" (They claimed that they wanted their incentives aligned with the company's and repeatedly rebuffed the board's attempt to raise their salaries.) "No, I think it's pretty cool that they only accept a dollar." "Cool" was the operant word—over and over again. I tried my best to foment discontent, but there was none lurking there—at least among the employees I spoke to. (Maybe these folks don't suffer from fraud anxiety, either?)

Perhaps this occupational cheeriness is a generational thing; or maybe it's just inherent to working at a number one–rated company; or it could be due to the charismatic authority of Google's leaders. I don't know. Certainly, traditional lines of authority are not as readily apparent at Google as they are in the old economy firms. Each time I witnessed a superior instructing an inferior (for lack of a better word) to do something, it was said with that New Age lilt of a question that began peppering the indicative (as opposed to inquisitive) speech patterns of youth about a decade or so ago. Or sometimes it was just a straight-up question, asked with an apologetic cringe as if it really would be the last time that she asked him to do some work.

Whatever the cause of the cheeriness, I must admit that it freaked me out, in the same way that zombies in a horror film might. Or, more accurately, it felt a bit like Orwell's Ministry of Information in *1984*. And, of course, that's what Google is: our privatized Ministry of Information. Just imagine if a government agency expressed its declared mission of organizing the world's information and had become the one-stop shopping site for all the world's knowledge. Pretty scary; people from all political stripes—from right-wing libertarians to the ACLU—would probably take up arms. But when Google does it as a private company, we cheer and thank God it's free to the user. If the first dimension of power is to overcome resistance and enforce your will upon others (in the words of the social theorist Steven Lukes), then the ultimate dimension of power is to secure voluntary compliance without even the thought of resistance. Google's management must have been reading up on its British social theory—both the human resources division and the customer relations side.

Perhaps my sister should take lessons in order to better manage her babysitters. She has calculated that after taxes and paying someone to watch her two young children, she nets somewhere between one and two dollars per hour by going to work. She continues to work, however, since she knows that her job is quite flexible and that soon her kids will be in school for most of the day, so she doesn't want to drop out of the labor market for fear of not being able to get back in. This choice has led to a number of distressing encounters with caregivers. Her first babysitter had to be fired after suspicions of neglect arose thanks to reports from other sitters in the park. They were confirmed after she and her husband rented a nanny-cam and looked at the most difficult footage they had ever viewed, crying as the sitter swatted their one-year-old son, pushed him away, and left him unsupervised for long periods in another room. Needless to say, they fired her immediately.

Time passed, and my sister decided to try a nanny again. This time, she hired someone she had known quite well for several years—the nanny for her best friend's children. It was serendipitous that the friend's kids, a few years older, didn't need a sitter anymore, so she could switch over to my sister's two children.

Celia was an excellent sitter, but that created a new set of problems. Before long, she assumed moral domination over the family, judging my brother-in-law for not spending enough time with the kids, scolding my sister for not maintaining the consistency of routine that she strived for during the daytime hours, questioning their dietary choices, and so on. It got so that the parents became afraid of the judgment of their employee, who they and their children adored as the perfect nanny. (The moral: Beware of Mary Poppins.)

As I've said, the relationship between authority and legitimacy has been inverted here, and in the process, class relations are radically altered. It's left to the toddlers to figure out and internalize the new social map, so by the time they are adults, this modern version of class relations will feel completely normal.

But because this new relationship often clashes with the legal-rational ethos of decades past, it can sometimes precipitate serious conflict. The old-school boss in a large corporation instructs his secretary, rather bluntly, to bring him his black coffee—no sugar—the first morning she is at her new job, and adds that she should have his letters typed by noon. But because he doesn't say "please" or "thank you," or offer to refill *her* cup when she needs more java to keep going, she gets offended. He has "disrespected" her. Gender and race differences between the two of them only exacerbate the problem: He was acting impersonally with assumed legal-rational authority, and she, instead, has been reared in the new economy of respect, where euphemistic job titles and pleasantries do their best to obscure huge earnings differentials, and where fraud anxiety–induced guilt about those inequalities regularly serves to invert power relations at the person-to-person level, as a sort of consolation prize to those at the bottom.

However, the erosion of authority doesn't necessarily mean America lacks cohesion or that our society is crumbling before our eyes. Indeed, we're held together fast by, of all things, inequality.

According to the highly stylized account of Emile Durkheim (another sociologist from the turn of the twentieth century), there are two general ways that communities hold together. One is *segmental solidarity*—cohesion based on sameness, like the segments of a worm. This form of collective life dominates, according to Durkheim, when each household is relatively self-sufficient and undertakes more or less the same activities: subsistence farming, a bit of cottage industry, and so on. Think *Little House on the Prairie*. In that kind of world, there is a premium on going with the group flow. Deviation from traditional norms is met with severe social sanctions (perhaps a scarlet "A" or a day in the stockade).

This stands in contrast to *organic solidarity*—cohesion based on mutual dependence and specialization, or what we used to call division of labor. None of us could survive, or at least live well, without one another. In Durkheim's time, the smithy needed the farmer who needed the shepherd who needed the glassblower who needed the teacher who needed the doctor, and so forth. People knew how to do *different* things from one another and were better off collaboratively than if each of them had tried to do all jobs themselves. This mutual dependence of all upon all created a sense of social solidarity, which tolerated difference and which sanctioned individual violations through "rehabilitation"—that is, trying to turn offenders into "productive" members of society once again.

Today, however, with our basic material needs taken for granted, we don't produce products but rather "service" each other like so many bonobos grooming all day long, so we are not held together by mutual dependence for survival. In an ironic twist, the inequality-induced economic red shift fills that role. This trickle-down economy (once a derogatory caricature of Reaganomics) is actually working, at least for those lucky enough to find themselves in the top half of the income distribution. That is, many professionals are doing better than they were before and, what's more, they have rich people to thank for that. The dean needs the donor. The entrepreneur needs the venture capitalist. The hedge fund manager needs the super-rich investors. The lawyer or the management consultant needs the corporate client. The doctor needs the lawyer, management consultant, and entrepreneur. And the masseuse needs all those folks to earn her livelihood.

So, neither she nor the professional dog groomer nor the

closet organizer nor the private tutor nor the organic foods consultant can rail against the incomes at the top. They depend on them even as these very same high earners induce that anxious feeling of falling behind. The growth in luxury services has been outstanding in recent years. The leisure and hospitality industry has grown by almost 30 percent over the past decade.[3] These are not just minimum-wage laborers we are talking about. They are often "professionals," whose entire occupation depends on a class of folks who can afford to shell out $200 per day for "doggie day care" or $75 per hour for closet counseling. In turn, the folks who service the folks with the big money themselves support other, less tony dimensions of the service economy. They may be doing well enough to hire cleaning ladies to make their porcelain sparkle. They may have money enough to hire a nurse's aide to be a companion to their aging grandmother in Scottsdale, Arizona, so they don't have to be there themselves. Or they may just be able to afford the basic services like DirecTV, broadband, a family cell phone plan, and Holiday Inn accommodations that are the markers of middle-class status. Those in the bottom half of the distribution chain work for the upper half as nursing assistants, taxi drivers, burger flippers, Wal-Mart staff, housekeepers, and so on. They, at least, get to buy cheap *stuff* at Wal-Mart, Costco, and Kmart—when times are good. When they aren't, it's these folks who suffer as the top scales back.

In other words, most Americans at the bottom end are not materially deprived in the classic sense of the word. Think Africa—that's not what poverty is like in the Bronx, the poorest urban county in the United States; or in rural Louisiana, the poorest state in the nation in 2006. Unlike starving Africans, in our country, lower-income folks eat; they just eat junk. Former senator Phil Gramm, a Republican from Texas, once boasted, "We're the only nation in the world where all our poor people are fat." America's poor have TVs and cell phones. They just have acquired enormous debt to get these things. Though prices are rising, food is still relatively cheaper than it has been for most of history. Even gasoline, despite a recent spike in oil prices, is not terribly more expensive in real dollars than it was in 1980—and it is kept cheaper here than anywhere else in the developed world thanks to a very low tax rate at the pump.

Poverty in a post-industrial economy is less about the ability to meet basic material needs and more about the lack of control over life choices and the personalized humiliation that the poor experience in their work lives. For example, whereas the middle-class lawyer may find it fulfilling to keep working a few days a week after the birth of her first child since she considers her work a rewarding part of her identity, the Wal-Mart cashier may like nothing more than to take her low-prestige job and shove it once she becomes a mother. If we lived in a prior epoch where the economic imperative was to earn enough money to buy basic material goods, then the decision of the lawyer would have no impact on the decision of the cashier. However, in a post-industrial service economy, where most of us are working not for basic survival but to acquire an ever-expanding basket of goods and services, and where most of the highly valued prizes are inherently limited by their nature as relative status markers, then the cashier has no choice but to keep working in order to try her darndest to keep up her family's relative income. Add in the fact that her job involves interacting with people all day long in a highly constrained way—acting pleasantly subservient is the nature of the game in the lower-wage service sector—and you start to comprehend the social nature of poverty in the post-material age.

Some on the left wonder why there is not more of a backlash against the high (and rising) degree of income inequality in the

United States. But it's really not too bewildering. It's because we are all implicated in the greatest Ponzi scheme history has ever witnessed. We all have to buy into this economic pyramid to keep it running. And since many of us enjoy decent, long-run returns on our 401(k)s—while simultaneously afflicted by fraud anxiety—we tend to go along with the program and hope it all works out in the end.

The result is a neofeudal economy, an economy of financial lords, vassals, and serfs. And it is an economy in which economic relations have become intensely personal, since services tend to be, well, personal by definition. Back in the nineteenth century, the German philosopher Georg W. F. Hegel observed that while we tend to think of the slave or servant as being completely dependent on the master, it is in fact the case that the master is equally dependent on the slave. He no longer knows how to clean his own toilet, walk his dog, trim his fingernails, or darn his socks—he is less than a whole individual. It is this master-servant dialectic that holds the intravaduals of the trickle-down, Elsewhere Society together. My sister and her nanny would not like to think of their relationship this way, but Hegel described the glue that holds them together almost two hundred years ago.

Convestment

The Way We Earn and Spend

Back in 1976, Fred Hirsch put his finger on one of the essential paradoxes of consumption in the post-industrial era. In earlier epochs, economic production was based on fulfilling basic *material* needs for survival. However, as we entered what some folks have dubbed "late capitalism," an increasing amount of economic activity is now devoted to fulfilling social-psychological needs. Ronald Inglehart called this "post-materialism," in his 1997 book, *The Silent Revolution*.[1] The critical issue is that an increasingly larger share of the goods or services we produce and consume in a post-material economy are what Hirsch termed *positional goods*. This type of good is distinct in that its value depends on the fact that others don't consume it.[2]

Certain goods are inherently positional: A penthouse apartment is, by definition, a positional good since there can be only one top floor per building. So is a beachfront property, given the limited supply of coastline. Others depend on group social dynamics to attain positional status. Platform shoes at a crowded rally are a positional good, for example, to the extent that they serve the purpose of giving us a better view of the stage. But if everyone wore them, the initial purpose would be defeated. (They still might look cool, of course.) A gun, in a sense, is a positional good, too. That is, a firearm is most valuable when nobody else has one. The same is true for education—at least with respect to degrees. When everyone has a certain level of education, the value of that degree diminishes. We see this already for high school diplomas, which no longer guarantee their holders much in the way of financial returns, partly because almost everyone gets one eventually. And though witty, Andy Warhol couldn't have been further from the truth when he predicted that everyone would enjoy fifteen minutes of fame in the television era. Fame is perhaps *the* quintessential positional good: If everyone gets fifteen minutes of airtime, then it is the guy who has a full hour (or the highest Google page rank) that's famous. Anything that provides *relative* social status or advantage falls into this category since the very value of the good is based on its exclusivity.

In 1958, in anticipation of Hirsch's fully fledged argument made eighteen years later, Sir Roy Harrod "pointed out that many of the advantages of being rich lie in the services that a wealthy person can afford—the bowing and scraping, the personal attention, the special treatment available to him."[3] However, in order for the wealthy individual to command such personalized goods, it is not simply enough that she be wealthy by some absolute standard. It is necessary for her to have significantly *more* resources than others in the society—in other words, it rests on inequality since the wages of the folks who will be doing the bowing and the scraping must be low enough for them to be induced into such an occupation as personal scraper. The essential character of positional goods in our time is that the satisfaction they provide is not *intrinsic* to their value to an individual—i.e., their ability to satisfy hunger, thirst, or even to express ourselves. Rather, their utility relies almost entirely on their relative *social* position. In this way, many of the goods we consume reflect the same interpenetration of the social into the self—colonizing, slicing, and dicing the modern notion of distinct personhood into the multiple selves (each linked to an external reference group) of the intravidualistic era. The same product—the penthouse apartment, for instance—may elicit joy and pride or sorrow and shame depending on whom we're having over for dinner, the neighbors who live down below us, or alternatively, the friends whose own penthouse is twice the size of ours.

However, it may be worth pointing out that an economy in positional goods does not need to wait for basic material needs to be fulfilled in a majority of the population. Many extremely poor but developing countries today have high levels of inequality. The fact of people desperately needing money for food often creates a very strong incentive for them to offer personal services. Think child prostitution. Nobody wants their child to sell his or her body, but sheer material poverty forces some families into offering that service. When I lived in Egypt and Pakistan in the early 1990s on very meager wages by Western standards, I was still able to afford a plethora of services I have never enjoyed since. I had my first and last manicure and pedicure in Cairo. I enjoyed my only scalp massage in Peshawar, Pakistan. In those tribal areas of Pakistan where Osama bin Laden is reputed to still be hiding out, I was advised that you could hire someone to kill an enemy for around $80 at the time (1992). Even more than fame or maid service, contract killing is the most drastic illustration of the positional good, since there is an inherently limited supply of targets—especially as the number of contractors increases.

So, positional goods have been with us probably since the days of cave people. The problem becomes that as basic material demands for survival are satisfied, more and more people demand positional goods, creating an untenable situation. This is the situation America and much of the developed world found itself in after years of postwar growth. This, too, is an important component of our economic anxiety: the worry that we will fall behind and become one of the maids scrubbing the toilets of rich folks and not the one having our porcelain shined.

Add in the fact that service is often personal (if not quite sinking to the level of the proverbial bowing and scraping), and you've got a toxic mix. The other day I took a co-worker out to a farewell lunch in an upscale restaurant. Everything was on autopilot until I turned to our waiter to ask whether the lasagna had meat in it. Suddenly, I was taken back twenty years to a college road trip gone bad. It turned out the waiter was an old friend. He, I, and a third dorm mate had rented a car and pulled a Jack Kerouac during spring break—racing (and I do mean racing) up and down the coast of California. Though we had some mutual friends, he and I had drifted apart for most of the intervening time. So, in between bringing our drinks and taking our main order, we reminisced a bit.

He congratulated me on the publication of my books, which he had read about, and on my children. He was still single and working at this restaurant twice a week, hoping to save up enough cash to start his own bar. These exchanges already made me feel uncomfortable: We had both started out at the same elite public university, and now he was waiting tables and I was being waited on. Maybe this is just a case of a nerdy sociologist who is overly class-conscious and suffers from a particularly large dose of fraud anxiety. Or maybe it's a more common experience today in an increasingly unequal service economy. When the conversation turned back to ordering, an even greater awkwardness descended on the table. What we were experiencing was role conflict: We had a personal relationship that should have trumped or precluded the hierarchical professional one of waiter-diner. However, we had to get on with the business of lunch, too. That uncomfortable feeling returned each time he refilled my glass, and I said a few too many solicitous thank-you's. At the end of the meal we exchanged numbers, I left a whopping tip, and then decided I would never return to that restaurant despite the fact that the food was fabulous.

In his nineteenth-century masterpiece, *The Philosophy of Money*, the German social theorist Georg Simmel argued that modern society has gone through an evolution of sorts in payment schemes. First there was "in-kind" payment. For example, a serf received some food and shelter for tilling the soil. He or she wasn't much different from the oxen who were fed and stored for the night. Basic human needs were taken care of, but the dependence of the worker on the largesse of the master was, in Simmel's view, dehumanizing.

Then there were the "good old" days of craftsmen and cottage industry, when workers were paid on a per unit basis. That is, you agree on the price for, say, a chair. The furniture maker procures the raw materials, fashions the chair, and delivers it on spec. If the wood is rotten, or he makes a mistake and has to start over again, there goes his profit margin. He bears all the risk. His wages are dependent on the quality of the capital goods. One step up the ladder from per unit payment is hourly wages. While many social theorists (most notably Karl Marx) saw the advent of wage labor as something to be mourned, Simmel saw it as a further step toward worker liberation. Now the worker was privileged over the raw materials. If the wood were rotten, and the chair turned out to be no good, the worker got paid all the same. Even better is a salary. Now the worker is not even dependent on how much work there is to do. His salary is based on what the employer thinks is a reasonable standard of living for someone occupying that kind of position. Best of all are honoraria and grants.

However, today you cannot order a coffee, buy a bagel, or pay for a photocopy without being asked to leave your change behind for "better service" or, alternatively, "good karma." The expansion of tip jars to every service establishment seems to march onward independent of the state of the economy. In good times, the supply of tips may be greater and thus drives their spread. But during recession, demand may increase as low-wage workers rely on tips more than ever, and thus the proliferation of jars continues unabated.

One way to view the spread of the tipping culture is that it represents the triumph of the free market. The promise of 15 percent (or more) may spur better service through direct economic incentives. This view rests on a number of assumptions, however, most notably the promise of repeat business. After all, why tip a taxi driver when you are about as likely to get him again (and have him recognize you, the "big tipper") as to find a pot of gold on Sixth Avenue? And why would I leave my friend a huge tip when I was simultaneously vowing never to return to that eating establishment?

If we subscribe to Simmel's hierarchy of payment schemes, tips are a big step backward and embody better than any other economic manifestation the ethos of the new feudalism in the service economy. It is already bad enough that service workers are programmed to wish us "a nice day" and to plaster a perma-grin on their faces from the moment they show up to work. The imposing tip jar further muddles business and sociability. If the promise of a dollar in the jar is what compels someone to be friendly, then does that not cheapen smiles in general? Conversely, how can service workers and customers be on equal footing if the cashier's livelihood depends on the largesse of the person ordering the mochachino?

The presence of in-your-face money not only hurts the relationship between the customer and the service worker, it also damages the relationship between the worker and the firm. Tipping creates what economists term a *principal-agent problem*. In other words, it creates different incentives for the worker and the owner of an establishment. A waiter whose income largely derives from tips is more likely to give an extra scoop of ice cream to a customer. Research shows that these kinds of acts do increase tips on average, but they, of course, cut into the profit margin of the ice cream parlor.

More important, tipping is not good for the workers themselves, either. While often tips may appear to be tax-free revenue, they create a high degree of income insecurity. Public opinion research has shown that most customers would prefer that service workers were paid better wages and thereby the need for and practice of tipping could be eliminated—as in much of Europe, for example.

So, in light of research and public opinion that casts the expansion of tipping and tip jars negatively, why the proliferation? Again, while the lack of official statistics makes any analysis nothing more than educated conjecture, my guess is that the proliferation of tip jars is at least partially the result of rising income and wealth inequality in the United States. While the rich get richer, those who serve the rich are increasingly left to appeal to the better instincts of the well-off. The rich also need to have a guilt-release valve. If they tip big, then how bad can they feel for driving their $40,000 SUVs and drinking their four-dollar lattes? (Of course, often it is the less well-off who tip the most, perhaps out of some combination of insecurity and greater ability to empathize with low-wage service workers.)

The cruelest irony is that the worst-paid jobs do not even afford their workers the option to garner tips. The men and women who take the orders and bus the tables at the McDonald's and KFCs of the world earn minimal (if not minimum) wages, receive no health benefits, and cannot even ask for tips. Also in this category of the untipped are maintenance and domestic workers, dishwashers, security personnel, and many other hidden service workers who work so hard to ensure that we "have a nice day." In fact, at one time, McDonald's allowed the practice, but the managers pocketed the money. When the public discovered this, outrage boiled over, and tipping was banned. So now it is only the employees in the middlebrow and high-end service establishments—ranging from Starbucks (whose employees at least get health insurance) to the funky coffee shops it competes with—who are able to paint the side of a sugar canister in bright letters asking for donations.

As long as folks demand positional goods in an arms race of sorts, society becomes a tinderbox—since the post-materialist desire for control over other people's labor is not highly compatible with democracy. There are several solutions to this problem. One is to collectively decide on restraints: If we choose to limit the growth of income inequality, then folks will have to just live with the fact that they won't be able to afford to buy someone else's labor to watch their children, clean their toilets, or massage their bunions. We in the United States have clearly not chosen this option. A second possibility is that we open up our economy more and more. This we have done. As long as we have a constant flow of low-wage labor—legal or illegal—coming in from south of the border, then more native-born Americans can afford gardeners, nannies, or personal trainers. Third, we can live in a state of constant flux with respect to relative position, as long as we have a forum for its expression other than human-to-human services. In other words, we can—like an expansionary sports league—imbue more and more aspects of life with a positional element. So things—like meals—that once were produced and consumed in order to satisfy a basic individual human need can sometimes become positional goods, too.

One consequence is the increasing role that material goods play as positional goods—something Hirsch didn't consider. Mrs. and Mr. Elsewhere absolutely have to have the latest iPhone, McMansion, or SUV. There's nothing inherent about an iPhone that makes it a positional good. Some (but not all) of its features are material improvements on previous models. It *may* save us time and effort to have all of our music, phone numbers, and photos in one handy little gadget. Or it may not, as some users are finding. However, to the extent that the pleasure from the iPhone or the Hummer or the $5,000 gas grill (a favorite example of the economist Robert Frank in his related book, *Luxury Fever*) stems from the fact that it is better—or at least more costly and thus rarer—than the grills of one's neighbors, it has become a status or positional good. It is through this magical endowment of material objects with the powers of relative position that we think we have solved the problems inherent in mass consumption of positional goods—if only fleetingly. Never mind the credit card bill that is to come: For now, the magical object has done its job, and we are satisfied (if not quite happy, since the actuality of the thing may be disappointing compared to the idea of owning it in the abstract). So, when people talk about the dematerialization of the economy, what they should be really calling it is a de-necessitation of the economy, as in a deemphasis on basic, physical necessities; or, alternatively, a luxurification or positionification.*

This view of the role of goods and services in the new economy stands in sharp contrast to that offered by folks like Chris Anderson, for example, in *The Long Tail: Why the Future of Busi-*

---

*A luxury has a precise economic definition: It is a good (or service), the consumption of which rises proportionately more when income rises (the amount of necessities we consume also rises with income, but to a lesser extent, while consumption of an inferior good actually declines when income rises as better substitutes are afforded). No goods are inherently luxuries, necessities, or inferior.

ness Is Selling Less of More. In this book, Anderson argues that the shelfless nature of online, centralized distribution means that niche markets have replaced blockbusters as the most effective way to sustain a profit.[4] Specifically, in the old days when the number of books, videos, or records that a given store could carry was limited by physical shelf space, consumer choice was limited. This situation has been elegantly captured in Tibor Scitovsky's classic *The Joyless Economy: The Psychology of Human Satisfaction* (no wonder he found the economy joyless, it was the 1970s after all).[5] In this book, Scitovsky argues that mass production and marketing constrained the choices (and tastes) of the many, allowing only "eccentric" rich folks to be able to afford rare or unique products. Anderson claims that this tyranny has been lifted in the new economy, where there are no physical constraints to inventory so that everyone can live like an eccentric millionaire, ordering esoteric movies on Netflix, finding out-of-print first-edition books on the Web, and downloading obscure music on iTunes. Perhaps this is true for a certain class of goods—namely, cultural products that we consume privately on our iPods or DVD players. However, the positional aspect of other goods means that the long tail may actually be more like a long ladder that folks climb, each rung occupying a slightly higher status position. Little do we know that the tail—and the ladder—pretty much extend on forever. So, rising incomes won't help the situation. They just up the ante.

I mentioned in the first chapter that a historic shift has occurred with respect to work hours. The income effect of wages has become swamped by the substitution effect between wages and leisure. What this means is that as wages rise, we could theoretically afford to work less (the income effect) by using our higher incomes to "purchase" leisure time. However, the substitution effect countervails: When the price—i.e., the opportunity cost—of leisure rises thanks to our higher pay rate, then the scales are tilted toward working more, not less. For the first time in history, the substitution effect has triumphed on balance, leading to a situation where higher-wage earners work more hours than low-wage ones.[6] No wonder the biggest rises in inequality are happening at the top! In fact, this shift in the relationship between wages and work hours may be both cause and effect of economic stratification. Cause since those who earn more work more, thereby redoubling the gap. Effect since the greater degree of inequality we encounter as we climb the income ladder may be what feeds the shift in the personal valuation of work over leisure.

It may also be the luxurification that drives the Elsewhere class to work more and more, for everything else besides our own time seems to benefit from the income effect more than the substitution effect. Take, for example, the promise of the paperless office. Computer screens—particularly when combined with Adobe Acrobat—were supposed to have *reduced* our reliance on old-fashioned paper. Instead, our per capita use of paper rose and then plateaued in recent years at over 500 pounds per person per year.[7] The income effect strikes back: Evidently we like to print out lots of things we see on the screen. Likewise, despite the rise in sophisticated telecommunications that should allow for us to substitute distance communication via e-mail, phone, or even video link for personal contact, we actually travel more for business and have more face-to-face meetings than ever before.

All of these apparent paradoxes stem from the same economic fact: The income effect washes out the substitution effect. Thus, even though reading a high-quality pdf file on your screen is easier than ever before and should, theoretically, reduce the need for printing, the fact that we can access more and more documents than ever before (the effect of rising "income") overrides the smaller reduction we get through substitution. Similarly, telecommunications raise our social "income" by allowing us to communicate with more and more people. And the greater reach of our networks overwhelms the reduction in travel provided by the fact that we can video-chat or e-mail our friends and colleagues instead of going out for coffee in person. Anyone who has promptly responded to e-mail only to discover that it generates more knows this.

Of course, it turns out that even if we don't produce the stuff ourselves, we want to hold it in our hands. The number of physical bank branches, for example, has increased, not decreased, since the rise of Internet banking that was meant to make branch banking obsolete.[8]

Perhaps the greatest of the many ironies of the contemporary economy is that though we produce services and not stuff, we *consume* more stuff than ever. (Of course, it's all made in China.) As *stuff* has gotten cheaper and cheaper, we generally have consumed more of it. And gotten cheaper it has. Take toys: Today toys cost, on average, 59 percent of what they cost in 1993. Apparel costs 89 percent of what it did fourteen years earlier. The result of these price drops, according to the economist Juliet Schor, author of "The Social Death of Things," is straightforward: We buy lots more of this stuff. So much so that by 2005, the average American consumed 3,109 kilograms (6,840 pounds) of "stuff" per year—a rise of almost 20 percent just since 1998. And less than 5 percent of that total is for food and beverages (though these, too, have risen, along with rates of obesity).[9]

As recently as 1991 (as far back as Schor's data go), we each purchased an average of thirty-four garments per year. By 2004, that figure had risen to fifty-seven per year—more than one a week! Clearly, clothes are fulfilling some need or desire other than keeping us warm and our private parts concealed. Clothes serve psychological needs in all societies, from the hunter-gatherers of Papua New Guinea to the Google workpits of Silicon Valley. It's just that the social meanings change. At one time, Schor recounts, clothes were so valuable as to serve as a form of currency. Sweaters and shoes might be hocked at pawnshops when finances were tight, to be reclaimed when financial pressures eased. A suit or dress might be an heirloom—carefully mended and tended so as to be passed on to one's children. This is not such an old phenomenon. Many of my own father's dress shirts had belonged to his father. While there were, of course, emotional reasons to keep them, they were also, my dad claimed, of a handmade quality that was difficult (or at least very expensive) to match today. Like so many of our changing symbols, the social meaning of clothes, then, has transformed from a marker of family ties and tradition to one of relative social position in the present moment.* Of course, this transformation is not just limited to clothing.

The exchange of *stuff* plays an important role not just in social status differentiation but also in creating social cohesion. Like the potlatch of prelitorate societies—where material goods were exchanged in a grand cycle until they were thrown into the sea as part of a major ritual that promoted social solidarity—we now circulate more stuff than ever before. Yet even with all this buying going on, we are as alienated from the products and services that we buy as we are from the services we produce. That's because when products circulate through the medium of

*Since we are buying so much new apparel each week, we have to clean out our closets to make room for the new stuff. Thus, exports of used garments have also skyrocketed. Schor tells us that in 1991, we exported about 130 million kilograms of used apparel to the rest of the world (mostly African countries). By 2004, we were offloading 500 million kilograms—over 3 pounds of clothes per person—a typical load of wash weighs between 5 and 10 pounds. (See Juliet Schor, "The Social Death of Things," working paper, 2007.) What are we doing with the rest? Probably it is rotting in landfill. Of course, most of these garments

money, they lose an essential social function they had when they were part of a gift (or even a barter) economy. The "gift," wrote the French anthropologist Marcel Mauss a hundred years ago, has the essential character of embodying the spirit of the giver and creating obligations on the part of the receiver. Unlike a sale (AS IS—NO REFUNDS!), a gift is always essentially a loan. Hence the prohibition about recirculating or selling gifts—or the obligation to hang the (ugly) artwork when the giver comes over for dinner. It is not a donation that can be used freely by the recipient.

What's more, the gift creates a moral obligation to reciprocate, thereby binding the participants in an ongoing social relationship of mutual expectations. The market-mediated transaction, of course, has the opposite set of norms: Once you own something, you can do with it what you may. And caveat emptor, once the transaction is complete, the seller is not expected to have any obligation to the purchaser. Social interaction is fleeting. Solidarity is not generated. The moral logic is stood on its head. Think of how much more most of us value gifts that are handmade by the giver than we do those paid for in the marketplace and wrapped by the cashier at the store.

We may tend to think of gift giving as a special occurrence that—Christmas and birthdays aside—has relatively little significance in maintaining social solidarity in modern society (let alone postmodern life). However, if we use a more expansive definition of "gift" as any transaction outside the marketplace that is embodied with the spirit of the provider—a meal cooked for a tired spouse or hungry child in one's family, a careful read of a friend's manuscript, or even an hour spent listening to his

---

were not produced in the United States but rather in East and Southeast Asia, so they are getting quite a world tour. Little did I know at the time that I bought a pair of used blue jeans in the Rwandan open-air markets that I was doing my small part to balance the world flow of cloth.

problems—then when we "marketize" the provision of all those things (through restaurants, editors, and psychoanalysts), we lose a fundamental way of relating to each other.

No wonder we purchase so much stuff these days: Perhaps we are ever in search of that elusive relationship provided by the simple gift (and its anticipated reciprocity). But the cash nexus—as some folks called the market—is boundless. When you slap down your cash or credit card in front of the register, your money enters into an ether that flows throughout the entire world, tying you to everyone in that system at the same time (and, therefore, ultimately to no one). Put another way, if a gift to one person obligates one person to give back in a small, closed system of two, then paying for something in the marketplace sets off a system of "exchange" that ripples out (and back) ad infinitum. Economists have a phrase for this: the *multiplier effect*. They love the multiplier effect, arguing that monetized trade generates more trade, which, in turn, generates more wealth for everyone. However, the moral aspects of exchange are diluted in a pond as large as the modern-day agora.

Second, when markets penetrate every aspect of our lives, the "winner's curse" becomes a central experience of contemporary economic life. The "winner's curse" is what economists call the phenomenon in which the person who wins an auction has actually lost since, by definition, he has paid too much for the object under consideration because he is, perhaps ironically, willing to pay more than everyone else. The seepage of market forces into every corner of existence makes this problem rampant. Whether it is buying a knickknack on eBay, purchasing an airline ticket for the holidays, or accepting a counteroffer to remain with one's present employer, the satisfaction of the purchase (or job promotion) is ruined by the nagging feeling that we paid too much (or accepted too little). Since everything is negotiable and all terms are unique, and since a potentially better deal is just a mouse-click away, this new breed of American professional often experiences a letdown when a transaction is completed. Thus, many of them consume everything with an ambivalence that may not have existed in prior epochs. The value/price distinction has collapsed in the Elsewhere Society.

This rising tide of physical (and nonphysical) consumption also drives a sense of alienation and panic among the Elsewhere class. As there is more and more to consume, a sense of satisfaction is ever more difficult to hold on to for any meaningful length of time—something that the psychologist Barry Schwartz points out in his book *The Paradox of Choice*.[10] Just as we always know someone richer, we know that there is a better car, phone, house, or school just beyond our reach. If not now, then in six months. Since the arms race not only expands upward but laterally like brush fire to infect more and more realms of consumption that we once thought safe from invidious comparisons, we suffer from a sense that our lives are out of control. After all, the only thing we can't buy more of as we get richer is time itself—especially since it will cost more then, apparently.

There is, however, a positive aspect to the endless search for the perfect positional good. Specifically, sometimes in this quest for "distinction," individuals are led to try to give their totemic objects of choice a personalized spin, embodying them with particular knowledge or histories that bestow status on the owner. It might be the handbag fashioned by garbage pickers in Manila's slums: The fashion statement rests both in the political stand, of sorts, taken by the owner and in the pleasure of telling how such a bag was obtained (especially if one cannot yet order them online). Or it might be the ability to talk about wine "intelligently." Or maybe the simple wooden table that was serendipitously purchased at a roadside house sale when your rental car broke down in New Hampshire that comes with a great story about the old lady who sold it to you while being pestered by a presidential candidate seeking her vote in the 1992 primary. Or the willingness of the Prius owner to boast about the greatest mileage per gallon she has ever achieved with her hybrid car that she hacked in order to be able to recharge the battery from a wall socket. The point is that an era of cheap, mass-produced products can also, paradoxically, generate status and value among goods (or even services) that fall outside that mass market—and, in turn, help preserve local history, knowledge, and skills. That's because often in the postmaterial setting, the social value rests in the aura around the product with which we imbue it.

In addition to positional or luxury goods, there is another class of goods that has been on the march of late: network goods. At first blush, a network good seems like the opposite of a positional good—the more people who consume it, the better off all users are. A single telephone, for example, is not much use. When only a few people have telephones, they still have limited utility. But to the extent that the phone lines are not clogged, when everyone has a phone, the value of my own phone is greater, since I can now call virtually anyone. Just as a greater proportion of what we consume has a positional element today, the network aspect, too, of many goods has risen. The Internet, of course, is the ultimate network good, as is language itself (to the extent that we want to be understood by the greatest number of people), but this class of goods is not limited to communications technologies. To the extent that the utility of something relies on others consuming it, it has a network aspect to it. So, for example, to the extent that the pleasure of reading a Harry Potter novel is not intrinsic to the solipsistic experience of savoring the writing itself but rather to the talking about plot twists and turns with one's friends, J. K. Rowling has created a network good. Some consumption can, ironically, have both a network and a positional element to it. Take parties: It's not much fun to have the whole party to yourself—you need others to come to make it a party, in fact. But at a certain point, you don't want more folks to show up. It may not just be congestion effects that you worry about—the fact that it's gotten too crowded for your guests to reach the beer. It may also be that exclusivity has a positional value all its own. So, you are walking a tightrope of hoping that folks show up: the *right* folks, who by definition have to be limited in number.

Google epitomizes both the positional and networked aspects of this postmaterial economy in its revenue model. To the user, the content appears free. Yet unlike many of its competitors that went under during the early 2000s when the tech bubble burst, Google survived by co-opting a method of advertising that had been developed by Goto.com (now a subsidiary of Google's main competitor, Yahoo!). The principle was simple and initially seemed to solve the basic problem of valuation in the information economy: Do not charge advertisers a flat fee; nor even a charge per view; rather, charge them each time someone clicks on a sponsored Web link to visit the site that paid for the advertising. Better yet, don't even set a price. Just hold an auction—perhaps with a minimal price (Google's minimum is five cents per click-through). This allows for sponsored ads to vary in price according to the market, the particular niche in which they will appear, and the position on the page. (The actual formula is more complicated since Google takes into account the historical click-through rate and the "quality" of the page to which the link refers.) Of course, this strategy shifts the uncertainty about value to the bidders. But at least they have some data to go on, since they can tell when a purchaser comes to their Web site from a sponsored link much more easily than, say, they can know the effect of a billboard, a co-marketing strategy, or a TV ad campaign on sales of a given product.

So, when I search for "microarray analysis" (a technique for analyzing DNA or gene activation data), I receive a listing of the first ten of almost 2 million sites that are bordered by nine paid sites: one on top (the company that paid the most), and the others that border the right-hand edge of the results page. When I search for "Barbie," however, there are no paid advertisements. Perhaps this is because barbie.everythinggirl.com (owned by Mattel, who makes the actual physical Barbie doll product) is already the first page that comes up under the nonsponsored sites. Mattel knows that people looking for Barbie games and catalogues online are going to search on Google and then click through to their homepage, so why pay a nickel each time? By contrast, in product areas where there is no clear monopoly, it may pay to advertise in order to jump the queue. Searches for "Elvis" yielded four paid links—though not for the official Elvis Web site (elvis.com), which came in first in the page rankings anyway. A search for "recipes" resulted in eight sponsored links, ranging from Kraft Foods to "how to lose 15 pounds in 3 minutes" (presumably without hacking off any limbs). Pornography offers six paid links, and "sex," curiously, none, perhaps for a Google fear of being prosecuted as a net pimp? (If I search for myself, so to speak, no paid sites come up, but if I search on "sociologist," one does; I have no "Dalton Conley" competitors, but I do have competition in my identity as a sociologist.)

If you are popular—in other words, if you get a high page rank thanks to lots of other Web pages pointing toward yours within the category delineated by the search terms—then there is no need to pay for anything. But if you are trying to nudge your way into the top ten to get noticed, you have two options: try to game the Google algorithm (which evolves to outsmarting the gamers); or pay dollars. In this way, the abstract notion of network popularity—or rather, of positional status—becomes, like everything else, monetized.

Another aspect of the new economics can be seen in these Google AdWords: the blunting of competition. The mechanism behind the auctioning off of paid links to be billed on a click-through basis was not invented by Google but by the company Goto.com, which later became Overture Services Inc. A patent infringement lawsuit was brought against Google in 2002, a few months after it initiated what was to become its flagship revenue generator. In 2003, Overture was acquired by Google's main competitor, Yahoo!, who was also Overture's biggest customer. And in 2004, the suit was settled through old-fashioned barter: In return for a perpetual usage license, Google paid Yahoo! in corporate flesh (and I do mean flesh, since the Fourteenth Amendment bestows personhood on corporations). Specifically, Google provided Yahoo! with 2.7 million shares of Google common stock a few months before it went public. Thus, when, after the IPO, the price of Google stock rose from the offering price of $85 per share to a peak of over $500, one of the happiest entities was that company's main competitor.

To recap: The inventor of the signature revenue-making product of the Web economy is bought by its customer. In turn, the new owner makes peace with its (still) greatest rival by getting a piece of it. Just as the distinction between home and work has blurred, traditional boundaries between producer and consumer or between rivals no longer exist in this economy. In the words of one Google executive, "Why compete with companies when you can just buy them? Cool!" Let's all buy each other and then the stock prices will just keep going up . . . A new business ethic for the Elsewhere economy; it would seem that even corporations (which are legal persons, after all) have become intravidualistic, having had their selfhood interpenetrated by their social peers.

Shoot the Moon

Public Life in an Age of Private Markets

In 1997, I was sitting on the floor of an apartment in San Francisco, surrounded by a bunch of new friends whom I had met through my soon-to-be wife. This was a motley assortment of artists and tech-geeks and some folks who were both. There were paper millionaires as well as urban squatters who subsisted on less than ten dollars a day. One particularly brilliant woman, an optical engineer (a holographer, to be more precise), was talking about a project that she hoped to pull off sometime in the not too distant future. She was already responsible—in my book—for one of the most incredible ideas never to have been prototyped: holographic laser brain surgery. By custom-fitting a laser hologram, surgeons would be able to burn out a brain tumor in otherwise inoperable spots, without even having to make an incision. In other words, a hologram allows the surgeon to pick a point in three-dimensional space where the intensity would be great enough to destroy tissue while having no substantial effect on any other point in the brain space.

Given how impressed I was by this invention, I was particularly eager to hear about her other *cool* idea. But when she told me, I was horrified. She claimed that she knew of a feasible way to project images onto the moon so that they'd be visible from the earth.

"You can't do that, Mary Lou!" I practically shouted, jumping up and almost knocking over my cocktail.

"Why not?"

"Because the moon should be left alone." I was pacing now.

"What?" she cocked her head to one side. "I would just do it once; we could project a peace sign or something like that?"

I took a swig of scotch. "I trust *you*," I explained. "But then everybody else will follow. It's just like Hiroshima and the bomb."

"No, it's not."

"Yes, it is. You must never tell anyone of this idea!" What I feared, of course, was the ultimate billboard, which I knew the moon would become if Mary Lou uncorked the bottle with her technical know-how. I suppose a legitimate argument could be made that if a world organization—say one dedicated to ending hunger or stopping global warming—were to receive the funds for the rights to advertise in thirty-second slots on the surface of the moon, then humanity could be better off. But what if my "reserve price"—the value I place on an ad-free moon—is higher than the price obtained in auction? What say do I have? And once commerce had encroached on the lunar surface, it would be difficult to reverse.

I am happy to report that Mary Lou has not—so far at least—projected anything on the moon. She has been too busy developing the hundred-dollar laptop for distribution in the developing world. Advertisements on the moon represent an extreme example of something that is happening more and more: marketing to captive audiences. Whether it's projecting advertisements in public spaces ranging from roadside billboards to the moon itself; or the proliferation of eating options at sports stadiums and other enclosed, monopolistic venues; the placement of vending machines and for-profit television in public schools; or the rise of Skymall, the airborne tchotchke catalogue, more and more of our daily lives are being penetrated by the manifestations of the market—namely, selling and advertising. Perhaps it is ironic, then, that New York City tries to enforce a law against panhandling on the subway, arguing that it's constitutional to protect people from hawkers or beggars in an enclosed (albeit public) space, when the city itself sells every inch of the wall space of those very same subway cars (and its buses) to corporate advertisers. The very concept of public space is collapsing before our eyes (albeit in slow motion).

First of all, there is the issue of the technologies themselves—the increase in people chattering away to "elsewhere" while walking down a city street or sitting in a park or driving down the interstate. Almost fifty years ago, the urban theorist Jane Jacobs wrote that "the eyes and ears of the street" were the basis of a community's social order—much more than formal laws, policing, and other government institutions.[1] Local residents kept a watch on kids playing stoop on the sidewalk. Shopkeepers noticed when suspicious characters appeared on the scene. Grandmothers leaning out of second-floor windows offered directions to lost tourists. Hence the importance of mixed-use neighborhoods. There are, of course, good and bad aspects to this sort of informal social control, but there is no doubt that it forms one of the bases of public order. Cell phones and iPods—not to mention the Walkmans and radios before them—tear at that social fabric by distracting the eyes and ears of the street.

Back in my childhood, the most notable impact was that created by the arrival of boom box radios to the city streets. The late 1970s witnessed a war of volume, as pedestrians—particularly in poor communities—tried to make their presence known. In my own childhood neighborhood, the sounds of disco could be heard echoing off the walls of tenements and projects for up to a kilometer. Often the music was so loud that it drowned out all conversation within a one-block radius. The size of the DJ machinery carried on mostly male shoulders seemed inversely proportionate to the social power that person wielded in society. Boom boxes—more derogatorily known as ghetto blasters—were a noisy form of social revolt, if one that was soon squelched by the powers that be. Mayor Ed Koch passed a strict sound law that cracked down on the blasting of music in New York neighborhoods. Other cities soon followed suit.

Then in the 1980s came Walkmans, presenting their own problems for urban social interaction. First there is the issue of safety: I can remember flinching many times as I watched a pedestrian step lively from the curb, bopping his head to the beat, oblivious to the bus barreling down upon him. I doubt that data are collected about how many people are hit by taxis, have their pockets picked, or meet other unfortunate fates due to the fact that they have tuned in and dropped out.

Now we have cell phones that combine some of the worst elements of the boom boxes and the Walkmans—in new and slightly different ways. First of all, cell phone users talk loud—louder than the mega bass of foam headphones. Many friends talk about their dread over the day that cell phone signals are integrated into the subway system and their only haven from the trivialities of others' lives (planes are next). When I first saw people walking and talking on the phone, I thought it was like witnessing someone brushing their teeth in public—a clearly misplaced private act. Obviously, the sense of public and private has changed with the technology. First there were phone booths. Then there were phone stalls that offered less privacy since they included only a shell of sorts with half walls and no door to shut. Then there were public phones attached to walls. And finally, private, personal phones—cell phones—with no physical barriers whatsoever between the talker and those around him.

This has at least two effects. First, cell phones are fundamentally different from iPods or Walkmans or even from boom box radios in their capability to annoy and distract others. They are even worse than hearing both sides of a conversation between two real-life people on the plane next to us. This is likely due to the fact that in overhearing one side of a phone conversation, we are placed into the role of the other, filling in the other half of the dialogue, thereby having our attention attracted by the pauses and interactional turn-taking that is happening in our midst.[2]

Arguably more important than the noisy neighbor on the park bench is the state of distraction into which cell phones put the users themselves. At least with Walkmans, people listened to music but their visual attention was still focused ahead. Maybe it's the fact that listening to someone speaking and talking back oneself requires a lot more focus than music does, but some cell phone walker-talkers are like a new form of urban zombie, completely oblivious to what is going on around them. This means danger for themselves but also for the blind man who is mistakenly wandering out into the street, for the little old lady who is oblivious to the predator casing her out, and so on.

Of course, not all cell phone users yell out what they had for lunch in crowded spaces. But one bad apple is enough to spoil any bus or train ride. Not all cell phone users tune out of their environment completely when they are on the phone, but many do. Some states have recognized the risks of multitasking when it comes to cell phones and driving, and have begun to pass a variety of laws to ensure vehicular safety. Community life is no different: There is a public cost to private goods.

Which brings us back to projecting on the moon: As Mary Lou told me of her plan in 1997, my mind flashed back to the decade before, sitting in a movie theater in New York, on the other side of the continent: *Do the Right Thing*. The film is still seared into my mind. Not because it was particularly powerful or a masterpiece (it was pretty good, but not mind-blowing, in my opinion). I remember it because of what happened before the film started. There was an advertisement for American Express. I was watching this Spike Lee movie in the Greenwich Twin Cinema (now retooled into the upscale health club Equinox, where membership costs more per month than rent for a one-bedroom apartment in many areas of the country, but that's another story). The crowd in the Twin Cinema back then was still a pretty political bunch—mostly leftover beatniks and other artistic types from the days when the Village was still the premier bohemian location in North America. So the moment that the ad aired telling these former hippies that "membership has its privileges," frizzy-haired boomers shouted and actually tossed things at the screen. "Six dollars for ads!" one man yelled. More than a few people got up and went to the box office to demand their money back. "Good for them," I told myself, as I guiltily sunk deeper into my chair. I knew they were "doing the right thing." In a moral compromise of sorts, I decided that I would complain on my way out. But I didn't want to miss the Lee movie about which I had heard so much. I resolved the dispute between my multiple selves by giving in to the desire to see the film. (In our affluent, Elsewhere economy, *guilt* is often the moral ax that serves to split our selfhood into intravidualistic fragments.)

The lack of ads at the movies was taken to be sacrosanct by us. After all, *we paid already*. We accepted ads on commercial television since we knew something had to pay for it as we weren't. (Never mind that television could have been conceived of under a different economic model, as the airwaves are after all public property.) But movies were already outrageously expensive. Yes, we had grown accustomed to, and even enjoyed, the previews. Previews were almost like getting to see extra, mini-movies in much the same way that newsreels and shorts provided the warm-up entertainment in a prior epoch. (Perhaps I should also lament the transition from short presentations to previews, but I am too young to be nostalgic over newsreels.) And, for many viewers, the trailers were the primary way that we learned about what was coming up. Films were generally not advertised widely on TV, and newspaper ads hardly gave you a good sense of what a movie was like. We also accepted those brief clips that exhorted us to get up out of our seats and march back to the concession stand to spend our money on popcorn, soda, and Jujubes. They were more like a public service reminder than brand advertising.

But an advertisement for a product (or rather, aptly, a service) that had nothing to do with the movie experience itself? That was outrageous, and violated what I'll call the "premium cable" norm: When you paid for extra channels like HBO, Cinemax, or Showtime (the big three back in the eighties), you weren't just paying for their content. You were paying for the right to watch *without ads*. That went double for movie theaters. Ever since they were the first air-conditioned public venues, cinemas were meant to be an escape from the rat race of Madison Avenue–driven capitalism, from the world out there where we were struggling consumers. It was supposed to be nice, cool, and comfy. What's more, we couldn't even change the channel in order to escape these interruptions of our viewing pleasure. Movies seen in the theater remain one of the few realms of mass culture that is often not consumed with split attention (though recently some folks have started turning the sound off their BlackBerrys rather than shutting them down, and continue to text with one eye on the big screen). Hollywood may be the most corporate, emblematic industry of the culture-based service economy, but movie theaters were an Edenic throwback to the days before air-conditioning was widespread in homes and offices.

Part of my rationalization for *Doing the Wrong Thing* was the fact that I forgave Spike Lee for allowing this to happen. The narrative that I had constructed in my mind began with the fact that Lee had reputedly financed much of his first feature film, *She's Gotta Have It,* on his American Express card. *She's Gotta Have It* is given credit for ushering in a new type of black cinema (superseding the by-then formulaic 1970s Blacksploitation genre) and is said to be among the first films to have ushered in a glory era in independent cinema (i.e., before Miramax blurred the line between independent and Hollywood). So he was, in my mind, giving Amex its shout-out as thanks for cutting him some slack during his directorial debut. In turn, I cut Spike some slack.

But I have never forgotten that first experience and am reminded of it each time an ad airs before a film. What is striking is how passively accepted such ads are today. No lawsuits ensued that first time; no petition drives (as far as I know); and never again did I see anyone get up and walk out of a theater. And I'd bet that even the firebrands who stormed out demanding a refund for *Do the Right Thing* probably eventually gave in and watched movies with ads. What are you going to do? You can't fight every battle, after all.

One way to view this development is that the private market is working. Nobody is forcing anyone to pay ten plus dollars to become a captive audience for advertisers. In fact, there are more options than ever before for the individual who is sick of high ticket prices and crappy movies. There's cable, Netflix, TiVo, Blockbuster, and YouTube. The quality of viewing at home—on large-screen plasma monitors or projection systems—is far superior to what it was back in 1989. And some might go so far as to argue that movie ticket prices have risen less than they would have in the absence of the revenue provided from the advertising (i.e., some of the savings have been passed on to the consumer in this competitive market).

That's all well and good. But there are those of us for whom the idea of watching *The Matrix* at home is not a viable substitute for the *experience* of getting away for a two-hour mini-vacation from ringing phones, screaming kids, and computer terminals. In fact, the very survival of the movie theater industry in the present era of 5,000 channels plus YouTube can be attributed to the appeal of getting out into a public space where our attention is relatively more fixed on the entertainment at hand than it is in other settings. So, to the extent that the demand for movies in theaters is relatively inelastic—does not change much in response to price changes—then consumers are not saving much by suffering through advertisements. Rather, movie theater operators—or more likely, film distributors—probably pocket most of that revenue.

A similar seeping trend has occurred in the distinction between commercial television and public television. One of the distinctive features of public television (or radio) used to be that it was free from commercials. Yes, there was always the biannual or quarterly fund-raising drive, during which the station repeatedly interrupted programming to ask for your donation in a tone that combined desperate pleading and motherly guilt. We accepted that as a necessary part of keeping public television and radio on the air in a time when government funding was always in danger of being cut back. However, slowly something changed. At first it was just that the stations acknowledged their foundation funders, as in, "This show was made possible by a grant from the John D. and Catherine T. MacArthur Foundation." Soon those one-liners extended to mini-ads, which extolled the virtue and missions of the donors, as in, "The Robert Wood Johnson Foundation, working in support of health and health care for all Americans." Then yet another line was crossed: Corporate sponsors were given the same "props," so to speak. Pepsico, Philip Morris, and McDonald's. What, then, was the difference between public and private television or radio? Yes, the ads were shorter on public TV, but the sponsors probably paid less in grants than they would have for airing a commercial on regular TV, and they were getting a tax deduction to boot. What's more, they were borrowing from the status of highbrow NPR or PBS—this might be particularly important to companies peddling stigmatized products, such as cigarettes. And, on top of all that, the targeted demographic was on average richer. Meanwhile, many PBS stations in the heartland were airing shows like *M*A*S*H* or *Leave It to Beaver*—formerly commercial content that migrated across the increasingly porous divide. Station managers were, quote-unquote, *just giving the viewers what they want* in a free market.

With the highbrow/lowbrow distinction increasingly moot, and the share of operating costs covered by taxes shrinking, what was really the difference between public and private on the airwaves anymore? The question becomes particularly salient when we consider that private, for-profit stations and chains are receiving public money—albeit indirectly—through the below-market licenses they receive for their portion of the broadcast spectrum. Of course, the issue may become moot in an era of broadband transmission over the Net. But only for TV stations. The electromagnetic frequencies are still worth more than ever—to cell phone companies, that is. In fact, in another example of a commons being sold off, the ultra-high-frequency

(UHF) television band is now being disbanded, so to speak, as the government pushes the remaining stations with channel numbers over 13 onto cable in order to make more space for mobile communications technologies. (In case you don't remember what UHF is as you are reading this, those were the channels 14 through 83 on the *other* dial that had little clicks in order to fit in so many numbers—already the numbers over 69 have been lopped off for cell phone usage.)[3]

The more important point is that our very preferences are altered through such slow but continuous change in the socioeconomic landscape. Stable preferences form the foundation of classic economic models. Allow each decision—individual or collective—to alter the preferences of consumers, and the result is a slippery slope into, well, anarchy; or, if not anarchy, then at least a really bad case of *path dependence*. If you want to know what path dependence is, just take a look at your keyboard and try to explain why the keys are arranged in the QWERTY format. The standard keyboard was arranged in order to slow down typists when typewriters suffered from a tendency to jam. Since we invested our collective human capital in learning to type this way, it was hard to change even when the jamming issue became moot and better, faster keyboards had been designed. And while we're at it, we could be on the metric system if it weren't for path dependence. The resulting "path"—dependent on starting conditions—is that we are at a lower "equilibrium" than we would be if we could break free of these historical chains. In fact, as our world becomes more interconnected through trade and telecommunications, path dependencies may become more widespread. Think of how English (bad English at that) has become locked in as a new lingua franca thanks to the Internet. Or how certain technical systems—such as GPRS data transfer over cell phones—get locked into continued use long after superior new technologies have been developed.

The issue of path dependence is also relevant to our present discussion of the public/private dichotomy (or lack thereof) since it is hard to get back public space once it has been encroached upon by private interests. It's easy to deface a blank wall or scratch the paint on a new car. It's pretty difficult to erase or repair them, respectively. A pit bull lets go of something it's got in its jaws easier than private industry will cede a property right back to the commons or public sphere.

This penetration of the commercial into hitherto unplumbed areas can be seen right in front of our eyes. Or rather, right below our noses: on our shirts, that is. Once upon a time, T-shirts were worn as underwear (which itself is a relatively recent, late-nineteenth-century invention). The twentieth century has been called many things; added to that list could be "the underwear century." It was during the first year of the twentieth century (1901) that the P. H. Hanes Knitting Company unveiled its catalogue of two-piece underwear meant to replace the one-piece union suit. The U.S. Navy, however, gets credit for the spread of the T-shirt into mass consciousness. Looking for a way to minimize the amount of chest shown by its V-necked uniforms, in 1913 the Navy issued sailors the since-named "crew-neck" undershirts that sported an elastic collar. (Meanwhile, the USC football coach outfitted his players with similar cotton, moisture-absorbing undershirts.) The T-shirt remained a way to spare our collared shirts from excessive sweat and odor for much of the first half of the century. But in 1942, *Life* magazine sported a photo of an Air Corps G.I. on its cover in *just* a T-shirt. The photo was not only striking for its brazen display of male sexuality—a man was shown in his underwear top, after all. But the shirt was printed with the soldier's unit. (As with the case of the Internet, mental health practice, and myriad other innovations, the military was the original source.)

By the 1950s, T-shirts had entered the political and cultural sphere in line with the growing informality that has been traced to the burgeoning youth culture of the time. Thomas Dewey, the 1948 Republican presidential nominee, followed by Dwight Eisenhower in 1952, battled Democrats by emblazoning their respective slogans across the chests of supporters ("Dew it for Dewey" was followed by the more successful "I Like Ike"). Meanwhile, Marlon Brando and James Dean made the (blank) T-shirt sexy. By the 1960s, T-shirt printing had diffused from presidential politics to the personal. The blank white undershirts were replaced by tie-dyed ones or T-shirts that sported generalized political slogans.

Commerce had begun to show its face on the fronts of people's bodies in this way as well during the 1960s. Mickey Mouse was a fairly common symbol back then. Budweiser featured a shirt with a can of beer printed onto it. And Coca-Cola made an early appearance. It wasn't until the 1980s, however, that the human torso became prime billboard space. This, too, resulted from an escalation of sorts. Most initial advertisements stemmed either from specific commemorations or from the clothing companies themselves. For example, during the 1970s, the black concert tour T-shirt became ubiquitous as a way for individuals (mostly teenagers) to signal to others that they had actually been there to see The Who in 1974 or Led Zeppelin in 1975. Perhaps this marked the fact that rockers could already sense that theirs was a waning genre. Who knew if the Stones would ever tour again, after all. The T-shirt might be worth something—if not financially, at least as a badge that proclaimed, "I was there, man." (Little did we know that the Stones would be touring well into their pensioner years.) Concerts were perhaps the most common, but by no means the only, one-off events that were fetishized onto cotton. The fact that you finished a 10K race or went to Key West was also worthy of splashing across your bosom.

Commerce seeped onto our chests, too, by virtue of the logos of the clothing companies themselves. It started with small logos on the outside of shirts. How shocking or comical our 1959 cousin might have found it to notice that we wore an alligator or a man playing polo on our breast as if it were a military citation. And in a sense, it was. What are we really proclaiming? We are shouting to the public square that we can afford Ralph Lauren or Izod Lacoste; in other words, we are asserting our position in the positional economy. (Hence the African-American urban fashion trend that began in the early nineties of not cutting the tags off clothing—leaving the rectangular labels that often come affixed to the cuffs of suit jackets, for example.) In a mass bourgeois culture, subtle signaling soon gives way to the sartorial equivalent of shouting. The result, by 1986, was that I proudly marched off to college in California wearing a Spuds MacKenzie Budweiser T-shirt. (Alcohol in any form, even as an auto advertisement, appears cool to a geeky prefreshman.) It turns out that I was not alone in my dorkiness: College students are prime targets for corporate T-shirt giveaways, since they not only get the opportunity to wear them more often than most folks in the working world (though this fact is, of course, changing as well), but they hate to do laundry, so a new T-shirt is always welcomed over schlepping to the basement laundry room with a stack of quarters.[4]

By the turn of the twenty-first century T-shirts had taken yet another shift, reflecting the economic landscape around us: They had become personalized, mostly through online vendors that offered more choices or custom-printing options. Perhaps it marked an improvement that T-shirts had gone from serving as a human billboard for corporate sponsors to sites of (semi-) individual expression ranging from the political ("Save Darfur Now") to the silly ("Without Me, It's Just Aweso") to the poetically painful T-shirts memorializing victims of gang wars. Here we see Anderson's *"long tail"* theory, mentioned in the chapter "Convestment," at work in a material object. Everyone can wear a T-shirt; informality and individual expression (usually from a menu of choices, of course) reigns. We have gone from being the billboard to being the product itself. (Progress.) T-shirts are just one of the cruder facets of the rise of a personal branding movement, which is what it sounds like: marketing oneself. Even the self becomes privatized and penetrated by the market in this way. It's a story of the long tail meeting the positional good: silk-screening in the cause of social distinction.

However, there is a tension inherent in this particular fashion system. In a materialist economy, status stems more directly from quality. It is easy to see, for example, how a suit made from high-quality merino wool will last longer than one made out of an inferior fabric. But in a T-shirt-wearing society, there is no obvious dimension on which status claims would be judged. Probably not the quality of the material—though to be sure there are differences in thickness between organically v. inorganically raised cotton and so on. It's more the coolness factor that matters. Is it vintage? What does the design look like? How witty is the shirt's message?

The blurring lines between private and public are not just about public space. They are about moral space, too. Take the case of McDonald's, which illustrates how path dependence can undermine our preference structure, our moral calculus, and even our basic way of thinking. From the first days that the McDonald brothers founded their eponymous restaurant in the

1940s in San Bernardino, California, on through the growing Ray Kroc empire, to the global behemoth it is today, customers patronized the eating establishment with the full knowledge and expectation that they were expected to go order their own food at the counter. They were not expected to, however, and generally did not, bus their own tables. McDonald's workers did that for them. But slowly, slowly that changed.[5] An ethic of individual responsibility took over in which more and more patrons cleared away their own refuse, to the point at which today when I see someone leave their tray, I get all huffy, shake my head, and think to myself, "Some people."

I, myself, feeling guilty that as a professional I make so much more than the average McDonald's worker, would never think of leaving my dirty work to them—especially when they seemed so short-staffed and harried. And I really get furious at my kids if they fail to respect others by not cleaning up after themselves. That's, of course, silly, I now realize. McDonald's is not a public park where we all need to pitch in to preserve "the commons." It's a private, for-profit establishment out to make money. The so-called market should take care of it. They just need to hire more people to keep the place spic-and-span, or else have customers vote for Burger King with their feet. Perhaps it was part of a secret plot: Hire fewer people in order to put pressure on the customer to look after his own garbage. At first folks might grumble a bit (just like in the movie theater), but eventually they would comply and adhere to some unspoken ethic of self-service in order to save McDonald's money.

Someone might argue that part of the value of not having to hire that extra shift worker to bus the trays and wrappers might be to save us a few cents on each burger. However, there is no doubt that most of the cost saving is going to McDonald's franchisors and the company's shareholders. The truly amazing part of the story is that the equilibrium holds. Even if *all* the cost savings were being passed on to the fast-food consumer, we still might expect folks to shirk. After all, how much money does it save me when *I*—one lone individual—actually clean up after myself? A minuscule amount—or rather, nothing, since I will have, by definition, already paid for the meal I have consumed. So, it's in nobody's individual incentive structure to clean up after herself. Yet many of us do it. In many areas of public life we can't manage to enforce norms of respect and stewardship of the proverbial commons—everybody's too busy looking out for number one. Still, for Ronald McDonald, the center holds; we all do our "duty," and the Franklinesque imperative of self-reliance drives a strong moral norm of pitching in.

Or take the increasing crossover between for-profit and non-profit ventures. Back in 1983, American Express (there's that pesky company again) inaugurated what would later be called *cause marketing*. This involves a partnership between a foundation seeking to raise money and a company looking to turn a profit. It's different—and in some ways more pernicious—than the sponsorship of public television by corporations. In the case of giving money to so-called not-for-profit broadcasters, corporations are seeking to buy credibility and moral stature. In the case of cause marketing, they are doing that while directly trying to increase sales by pressing the moral pressure point on the soft, guilt-ridden underside of the American consumer. American Express presaged Ronald Reagan's "Morning in America" 1984 campaign message by promising that for every purchase made with the charge card, the company would donate one penny to the fund supporting the restoration of the Statue of Liberty (never mind the implications of the fact that we needed to go begging in the private sector to take care of something that was government property—this was the Reagan administration, after all). The effort raised $1.7 million of the $62 million cost of the project.[6]*

Any economy is a moral system. That was something that Adam Smith recognized almost three hundred years ago. (He was, actually, a moral philosopher by training and the author of *A Theory of Moral Sentiments,* a book that was almost as important to philosophers as *The Wealth of Nations* was to economists.) And with the Amex–Lady Liberty campaign, our moral economy took a new turn. We must remember that in a post-materialist society, we don't really *need* most of what we charge on our plastic cards in any meaningful sense of the word. So there is perhaps—particularly among the upper echelons of the income distribution—a certain feeling of guilt associated with consumption (an annoying holdover of the nineteenth-century Protestant Ethic perhaps?). Cause marketing—whether led by Amex in 1983, or Gap's Product RED a quarter century later, which aims to donate a share of profits to African causes—acts as a salve on that annoying rash of ethical uneasiness as we consume. It presses so many preprogrammed moral buttons. As Gap's own propaganda proclaims, "This isn't charity; it's a new way of doing business."[7] After all, that vestigial Protestant curmudgeon inside all of us doesn't feel quite right about charity, either.

---

*Of course, we can't just blame Ronald Reagan. In the last Gilded Age of staggering inequality (ca. 1885), insufficient funds were appropriated for the construction of the pedestal on which the French gift—Lady Liberty—would stand. The newspaper magnate Joseph Pulitzer used his editorial pages to shame America's rich folks into donating more money to support the effort. And then he took his plea one step further by printing the name of every contributor, no matter how small the amount. A bit more than $100,000 was eventually raised through more than 120,000 contributions, and in the process, the circulation of *The World* increased by 50,000. So, it was actually Joseph Pulitzer who "accidentally" inaugurated cause marketing a century before Amex came on the scene.

Sometimes the linkages reach absurd levels, as when Robert F. Kennedy, Jr., launches a new bottled-water brand, Keeper Springs Mountain Spring Water, with all after-tax proceeds going to water conservation efforts. Never mind that bottled water is now more expensive, pint for pint, than gasoline when a free substitute exists all around us. Or that the bottled-water industry is one of the greatest environmental nightmares—particularly the plastic bottles themselves, which take over 10,000 years to degrade if the caps are left on. Or that it actually takes two liters of water in the production process to bottle a single liter. Or that it presents perhaps the most tragic case of privatization when water bottle vending machines are allowed into public parks and schools and the existing water fountains are left unrepaired. Or that for one tenth of the money Americans spend on bottled water in a single year while good, clean FREE water flows all around them, they could solve the problem for the billion plus poor people of the world who truly don't have access to clean water, making water scarcity and insufficient sanitation the number one cause of death for children under five in the world.[8] Or that there exist more health monitoring and safeguards for public water sources than there are for private bottlers.

The point is that, like the McDonald's tray bussing, we never have time to stop and think how we got here and what the alternatives are (or might have been?). No time, because we are so busy rush, rush, rushing through the Elsewhere economy. Perhaps we might support the Statue of Liberty and the Global Fund to Fight AIDS directly through donations or (God forbid) tax dollars? It would at least keep our notion of a coherent moral self intact. The merging of "wasteful" consumption with guilt-relieving charity in the same purchase act is yet another manifestation of intravidualistic self-splitting.

The self-splitting guilt running through the post-material society produces other paradoxes in our public, political sphere as well. For example, ours is a culture where best sellers such as Tom Frank's *What's the Matter with Kansas?* appear, wondering why "peasants" in the so-called heartland apparently vote Republican (i.e., for lower taxes and less redistributive spending) against their own economic interests; but it is also one in which nobody wonders what's the matter with Manhattan, where the richest 2 percent of the population routinely vote for higher taxes on themselves by pulling the Democratic lever. During the 2004 presidential campaign, the research firm Prince & Associates surveyed four hundred Americans who had net worths of a million dollars or more. As has been true for most of American history, those who were well-off favored the Republican candidate. But among those worth more than $10 million (what many people really define as "rich" today in a world of million-dollar two-bedroom apartments in some big cities), John Kerry outpolled George W. Bush by 59 percent to 41 percent.

Noblesse oblige, it seems, is back in style and drives much of our elite politics. Ours is a politics in which Warren Buffett and the father of Bill Gates, Jr., are the lead spokespeople for *retaining* the estate tax (though to his credit, Andrew Carnegie made similar arguments a century earlier). And then there is the rise of the "family foundation": 40,000 of them[9] helping to contribute to the fact that the United States enjoys $295 billion of private giving each year.[10] Our donations exceed 2 percent of GDP, and given the size of our economy, in raw dollar amounts we give more than the next thirteen countries combined.[11] Of course, keeping in line with its moral function, most of this goes to churches. We must never forget the spiritual dimensions of the economic system.

From Elsewhere to Nowhere

Crime and Punishment

Not all of the recent changes to our public and community lives are as bad as being trapped on a bus with a neighbor shouting on their cell phone about their last meal, or being stuck in traffic during a long commute with nothing to look at but billboard after billboard of advertisements. There is at least one important improvement to public life in the Elsewhere Society that has been well documented: the reduction in crime. Put more accurately, there has been a change in the nature of crime, both in what it entails and who bears its cost.

If you interviewed any criminologist in the 1960s and told him or her that inequality was going to rise dramatically over the course of the next four decades while "real" (inflation-adjusted) wages for the bottom third of earners would stagnate, ninety-nine out of one hundred of them would predict steep rises in crime. If you told them that communications technologies and marketing would reach a broader and broader public so that we'd all know how the other half (the upper half, that is) lives and, what's more, be told that we could "have it all," too, these criminologists would have doubled down their bets and said that there will be riots in the streets. They would have been wrong, of course, but they wouldn't have been crazy, or even irrational. That's because the reigning theory back then was that crime results when individuals with differing economic means are socialized into having the same desires. Yet with the arrival of the new economy, we've seen the steepest crime drop in recorded history.[1] What's going on here?

Perhaps we don't all want the same things, after all. Did the long tail solve the "equal wants" problem? Well, the long tail means that we might all want to download different songs on our iPods, or that everyone has a unique queue of movies on their Netflix accounts, but it doesn't get around the problem that we all want to watch movies or listen to music and that these things cost money. And, of course, we want lots of other things—more and more things and services—that cost more and more money. Meanwhile, wealth is becoming more and more concentrated in the hands of fewer and fewer families. No, the real issue is that what we want isn't so easy to steal.

But let's back up. Before I was born, my parents chained their black-and-white television to the radiator in their walk-up apartment. That, however, didn't deter the many thieves who climbed into their windows on a regular basis. It was the late 1960s in urban America—a time when the incredible postwar boom was in its twilight and inequality was at a low point before beginning its steady annual rise in each year since. During the sixties, expectations rose more quickly than did opportunity, causing frustration to pour out into the streets in the form of riots and crime. My parents (and later myself) were on the front lines of that unrest, living in a poor neighborhood of New York City. Mostly we just tried to hunker down and take preventative measures like the TV-on-a-leash.

When I was a kid, we routinely drilled a hole through the hood of whatever used car we had inherited from my grandparents in order to pass a chain through it, which we then fastened around the front grill. The lobotomy-sized hole in the hood was only one of the ways we decimated the resale value of the given automobile. The hubcaps would be stolen within the first week of our parking it on the New York City streets. Likewise, though we sported the ubiquitous NO RADIO sign in the window, it did nothing to prevent the A.M. band, push-button model from being stripped out. That, in turn, meant a broken window that needed to be repaired, of course, and it also meant that my sister and I had to be careful not to sit on shards of broken glass. Less frequently, we'd show up to the car for a family trip only to find that it was sitting on cinder blocks—all four tires having been stripped away. We could live without a radio, AC, or hubcaps; but when the wheels were stolen, it meant that we had to do some serious calculation—figuring out whether it was worth replacing them at great expense or if we should just do without a car until we received a new hand-me-down from the grand-parents.

We also could not live without a battery. That said, the chain through the hood worked, as it turned out: Never after my parents came up with this idea was our car battery stolen, whereas before, we had to replace it two to three times a year—often buying our original one back on the black market to which the cops directed us. It was a pity we had to ruin our American Motor Company Rambler, an already extinct U.S. make that folks offered us money for occasionally while we idled at red lights. The car itself—inherited from my unmarried great-aunt (the grandparents only bought GM/Ford)—was a symbolic casualty of the Treaty of Detroit. The last one was produced in the year of my birth, 1969.[2] So perhaps it was metaphorically appropriate that it fell apart in our hands, piece by piece, over the course of the 1970s and early 1980s. Though increasingly rusty over the years, our particular model lasted until Reagan took office; again, perhaps, a fitting date of expiry.

My mother tried to solve the crime problem at home, too— with mixed results there as well. We joined the NYPD's "Operation Identification" program. A couple of local officers came over to our apartment and used an electric stylus (a sort of tattoo pen minus the ink) to engrave a code number into our valuables. Thereafter, our TV, clock radio, even our toaster had my mother's Social Security number engraved into it; this "code" was intended to make it difficult for thieves to fence these items on the black market and/or easier for the cops to return them to us if they ever found them. At the completion of the task, one detective smoothed a bumper sticker across our steel door. It read: BEWARE: WE PARTICIPATE IN OPERATION IDENTIFICATION.[3]

This particular policing innovation failed to be effective, at least in our case. A few years later, burglars swung through an open window and walked off with our engraved possessions. When we replaced many of the items, whoever it was (or perhaps a new thief) crashed through our now locked kitchen window, leaving a trail of blood across the floor and down the hall as they hauled their loot out the front door and into the elevator. What's more, we lived on the twenty-first floor. Today, by contrast, what junkie, crackhead, or generic delinquent would risk his life by crashing through a window over two hundred feet above the ground to steal a few things when there is eBay to buy stuff at cut-rate prices? For that matter, what were *we* thinking back then? What nut in this day and age would engrave their Social Security number in public display—and link it to the home Zip code by virtue of the location of the objects and our name on the front door, to boot? Today, the Social Security number would be what we'd worry about losing. The stolen TV set would merely be the receipt. Perhaps new burglars look for doors like ours—advertising easy access to confidential information. They should. Russian identity-thefting mobsters are waiting on the line for their calls.

Sometime around the same period that we participated in this crime prevention program, I got into rock 'n' roll. Or rather, like almost every other pubescent American boy, I briefly thought I'd like to be a rock star. I decided that I needed an electric guitar and an amp (never mind music lessons). When I had saved enough for the amp, I wandered over to Second Avenue, which at that time served as the pawnshop district thanks to its short distance from the Bowery—the largest skid row in the Western world. I found an amp and purchased it. By the time I figured out that it was a bass amp—not suitable for the guitar I was saving to buy—I had actually lost interest in the whole boy band endeavor, facing the reality of my total lack of musical ability.

So there I was with a bass amp that had cost months of saving up. I did what any American entrepreneur from Ben Franklin to the latest hedge fund manager would do: I found a sucker to pawn my pawnshop purchase off on. It wasn't too hard, since I went to school in the richer part of town—a school where most of the kids never ventured over to the pawnshop district and thus didn't know what bargains could be had for a wide array of merchandise of dubious provenance. Akin to the Arab traders who traversed the desert with precious spices, or the East India Company that brought tea to Great Britian, I became a pawnshop arbitrager across a much smaller geographic divide. (And probably a dealer in stolen goods in the process.) The end result was that I sold my $35 amp for $50 to a bass player and ended up with a nice little profit for my brief, if nerdy, foray into the world of rock 'n' roll. I was to bass amps in the early 1980s what Enron was to electricity in the early 2000s. Today, of course, the Bowery is home to luxury condos and the pawnshops are almost all gone. The opportunity for bass-amp arbitrage has largely been rendered moot by eBay and UPS. The real trading opportunities are in the legal and illegal buying or selling of information, like my mother's credit card numbers.

But this is good news: One particular bright spot in the transformation to an economy of high inequality, pervasive markets, and cheap or immaterial objects is the reduction in—or rather, the transformation of—crime. Specifically, violent crime is less common. In 1960, as registered by the FBI, the total violent crime rate nationwide was around 160.9 (about 161 violent crimes for every 100,000 people). By 1992, near its peak, the number had soared to a little over 757.[4] There have been many explanations bandied about for the reduction in crime rates. Harsher punishment is one of them.

By 2002, a recent low point in crime rates, about 5.6 million adults at some point had served time in state or federal prison. That's about 2.7 percent of American adults, up from 1.3 percent in 1974, the equivalent of 3.8 million people. If these incarceration rates remain unchanged, then according to estimates, about one in every fifteen persons will serve time in prison at some point during their life.[5] Crime-fighting policy aside, this "nowhere society" of felons is really to be expected in an economy that has changed its expectations of workers so rapidly. What else are we going to do with all the folks who don't fit into the new knowledge economy? We can either give them welfare checks or lock them up; while it is perhaps more cost-effective to provide welfare payments, keep in mind that the prison-industrial complex doesn't just take care of the surplus, low-skill labor pool made up by the convicts themselves. It also employs prison guards and many other workers to keep watch on them. Whereas once states had to battle NIMBYism when they attempted to site prisons, now communities that have been devastated by the decline in the manufacturing sector often vie for the right to host maximum-security facilities and the jobs they bring with them.

At least two sites—McAlester, Oklahoma, and Angola, Louisiana—make prisons not just sites of economic growth but of cultural life by hosting Prison Rodeos. Condemned by some as cruel to animals and convicts alike, these extreme sports happenings include such events as Bull Poker, where convicts sit motionless at a card table (covered by a red tablecloth, no less) as an angry bull is sicked after them. The local crowds go wild and the convicts look forward for months in advance to the spring and fall Sundays on which the rodeos are held. Those inmates who'd rather not run with the bulls, so to speak, can participate in the Crafts Fair that runs simultaneously to the Angola Rodeo. They stand behind a chain-link fence as customers browse through their handmade wares set out on tables. When I went to buy a chopping board, the craftsman handed me a bill through the fence, which I then took to the main kiosk to pay. I brought my slip back to the inmate, who tore off his yellow copy (to claim credit for the money, all of which goes back into the supplies they are required to pay for themselves). I kept the bottom pink slip to show along with the item itself on my way out of the prison grounds. It is perhaps ironic that these men were now trapped into a subsistence, handicrafts economy, using tools and technologies that date back to precapitalist times. (Some inmates who have not yet earned the right to use tools fashion their wares completely out of paper and glue, going so far as to make full-sized, functional paper guitars.)

These men constitute the surplus labor that is not needed anymore now that America's factories have been converted to lofts. They are, for the most part, the undereducated class that has fallen too far behind to be rehabilitated (made productive again) in an economy where skill requirements seem to increase yearly even for those of us on the "outside." They are the "nowhere men"—the necessary, dialectic complement to the Elsewhere class. Yet they, too, suffer from the affliction of multiple selves; indeed, the language aging felons use to describe their crimes and misdemeanors is riddled with reference to the younger, stupider self who made the mistakes that landed the older, wiser self in prison. And this rasher, brasher self is never gone; it tempts and taunts and dogs its holder over years of "rehabilitation."

Conservatives (and some economists) like to say that this rise in the "cost" of doing crime—in the form of harsh sentencing—along with the effect of taking would-be perpetrators out of circulation is responsible for the dramatic decline in violence, and indeed in all types of crime. Others argue that the spread of community policing, whereby beat cops work the streets to *prevent* criminal activity rather than respond to it, is the prime reason for less street crime. An improving job situation during the 1990s may get some credit, too. Still others argue that demographic factors are what mattered: The proportionate number of sixteen- to twenty-nine-year-olds (the group most likely to commit crime) was in decline over this period.[6] Perhaps most controversial is the concurrent claim that legalized abortion reduced the number of unwanted children and therefore the number of potential criminals—followed closely by the somewhat parallel argument that the nationwide switch to unleaded gasoline has driven down crime since we now poison the developing brains of our (wanted) children less badly than we once did with our gas-guzzling vehicles.

Or perhaps property crime has gone down because there's nothing really worth stealing in the new economy. At the time I looked, there were no car batteries on sale on eBay. So, clearly, either they are being fenced in old-fashioned ways on the streets or they aren't being stolen much anymore. Rather, the search term "car battery" yielded lots of cell phone battery chargers. I have no idea how many of those were stolen, but since most were on the order of $10 ($2.63 back in 1973) and in new packaging, I hardly think they merited the risk. And since the inflation-adjusted price of an actual *automotive* battery has fallen drastically since 1973 (around the time when our car hood was first chained shut), I doubt that there are many back alleys or chop shops that are acting as fences for auto batteries. Back then, a typical battery ran $50, or about $200 in today's money.[7] By contrast, today most are in the range of $100–$200 (and last much longer, so are actually cheaper in terms of dollars per mile driven). Perhaps not really worth stealing then. Meanwhile, the speeding up of the fashion cycle—which shortens the lifespan of products and services before they are perceived to be obsolete—means that fencing many types of used goods is simply not as worthwhile as it once was.

What's more, the forbidden stuff that most criminals craved has gotten much cheaper. Long gone are the days of $100 per ounce cocaine as the only option ($400 in today's dollars). Crack offers a much cheaper high and stiff competition for the pure cocaine market, driving down that price as well. Ditto for crystal meth as well as many other drugs.

Perhaps I should give the benefit of the doubt to my childhood thieves. Maybe they weren't trying to get high and truly needed the money to feed their families. It certainly could have been possible in the 1970s, since food was something that cost relatively more back then, too. I remember once watching a woman try to smuggle two hams out of our local Pioneer supermarket by feigning pregnancy with the two cuts of meat protruding from her sweater. When they accidentally dropped out as she passed the store manager's perch, he announced to the entire store over the P.A. system: "Look, it's twins! Congratulations. Usually I see only single births in this store, but today this lady is having twins." He then detained her until the police arrived. I have no idea if the hams were entered as evidence or whether he stuck them right back in the meat and deli section. But since that time, the price of a calorie has dropped substantially: by about 36 percent (helping create, of course, its own social problem in the obesity epidemic).[8] In short, goods—even food—are just not worth the risk of stealing anymore.

Someone may counter that while prices have fallen for some goods in real terms for the average family, wages at the bottom have been stuck for most of the last four decades. Stagnant wage growth has been a mantra of Democratic politicians and labor activists for the past two decades. Yes, it is true that if you track median wages and plot them against price rises based on the official inflation rate—the consumer price index (CPI)—then it does look like real wages have stagnated for the bottom half for most of the period since the oil shock of 1973.[9] However, as my graduate school economics professor pithily stated: "Inflation is a great measure in the short run; but it's a lousy measure over longer periods."

That's the case mainly because of the way it's calculated. Basically, the U.S. Bureau of Labor Statistics takes a common "basket of goods" and tracks the changes in prices of those goods from one time period to the next. (This is an oversimplification, of course, but mostly true.) The problem comes in defining that shopping "basket," since what are considered common or basic goods shifts over time. My professor's favorite example was the cost of calculating 239,252 times 873,123 or other more complex math problems. If you think about the cost of calculations, they have dropped steeply since 1955, when most folks would have needed pencil, paper (or perhaps a slide rule), and a few minutes to arrive at the answer. Today, of course, the speed—the opportunity cost in labor time—which such an answer "costs" is trivial (it's 208,896,423,996, by the way).

That may be a rather esoteric or abstract way to think about the limitations of the official inflation rate; but think, for example, of the cost of new technologies. The award-winning economist Jerry Hausman argues that the Bureau of Labor Statistics is notoriously late in adding new products to its basket. It thus routinely underestimates price drops, and therefore overestimates the inflation rate. He gives the example of mobile telephones, which entered the consumer market around 1983. It wasn't until 1998 that the government got around to considering a mobile phone as part of its price calculations. By then, the average price for the phone itself as well as monthly service charges had dropped by over 500 percent.[10] Back in 1983, hardly anyone paid for the huge and clunky wireless technology, so perhaps we could forgive the government bureaucrats for waiting to see if these gadgets would catch on. But Hausman (and I) think that fifteen years is way too long. And it's not just mobile phones but lots of new technologies that get left out of price calculations. Never mind that the quality improves dramatically as the new technologies get better and better with each iteration.

Think computers, Gameboys, iPods, cable television, and the Internet itself, to name a few. This statistical insight about inflation helps us comprehend the very real sense that material standards of living for even the bottom half of Americans have actually improved. Some measures try to get around this problem by calculating labor time. Take, for example, *The Economist* magazine's "Big Mac Index," which compares the price of the famous McDonald's hamburger across the globe in terms of hours needed to work to afford one. Of course, what if you are a vegetarian? Or would do without a Big Mac in order to save up for a new iPhone? There's no easy way around the fact that our tastes and preferences change with the development of new products. The bottom line is that while there is no doubt that some costs have gone up (think housing), it is not really fair to say that standards of living for low-income families have declined. Rather, they have *changed*. The more serious, negative consequence of uneven growth for those on the bottom is that they have increasingly to service those on the top, experiencing all the social-psychological costs attendant to such jobs in order to afford their Nintendos and the like. Although such psychic violence may be a reason to riot in the streets, the relative improvement in poor people's material conditions—despite what official statistics about inflation-adjusted wages tell us— probably plays a greater role in explaining the declining crime rates of recent years.

Of course, it is also true that the rise of e-commerce simply makes it more difficult to mug someone. Today, thanks to credit and debit cards and the ubiquity of ATMs, most people don't carry much cash (proportionate to their incomes). (That said, it would seem easier to pick people's pockets these days, or just conk them on the head with a club like so many baby seals as they cruise down the street, clicking away on their BlackBerrys totally unaware of their surroundings.) You can still knock off a liquor store, but surveillance cameras, DNA identification, and other new technologies make that more risky, too. And violent crime flows from property crime. You are much more likely to end up shooting someone when you are robbing his liquor store than when you are selling his credit card number to an identity fencer.

If it has become harder to knock off a liquor store or a bank, just think how hard it is to rob real estate, transportation, utilities (phone, etc.), health care services, or education—even heavily armed. Those are the expenses, in rank order, that have taken over the largest income shares of American households. Housing has doubled in its share of household budgets since

1960 for the average American family, now constituting a third of monthly expenses on average.[11] The share of budgets for shelter exceeds half for lower-income households.

While transportation is costly for all income brackets, it is the upper-income earners who spend the most, even proportionately to their income. Poor families' number two expense is still food, but now most of that money is spent eating out. Then comes utilities, at 9 percent; health care, at 8 percent of budgets for low-income families; and education, at 4 percent for the bottom tier.[12] With the exception of food and perhaps a car, none of these are physical things that can be stolen (compared to the household durables that we had engraved back in the 1970s). Of course, you could steal the monthly rent or lunch money; but as we've seen, stealing cash isn't so easy anymore, and there's not much worth fencing. In short, a gun doesn't do much good when trying to rob a service in a weightless economy; it's like shooting at a mirage. What's more, even if you were looking for the oldest service from the oldest profession—paying for sex—you would probably do that online, too, now. Street prostitution has largely been eclipsed by Internet porn and solicitations.

Sociologists have long observed that in a given society there is generally a fixed level of deviance and that what varies is the elastic definition of that deviance. If we take as a given that there is just as much crime as there ever was, where did it go? Since each economy generates its own type of crime, then we should look to the new information, service economy to find out where the deviance is hiding. In fact, it's hiding in plain sight—in your inbox:

RE: TRANSFER OF USD 38,000,000.00 MILLION TO YOUR ACCOUNT

So writes Mr. Jan Mbaala, a so-called minister in South Africa who wants to channel embezzled funds from Iraqi oil sales into my bank account. Perhaps it is no coincidence that the typical criminal solicitation today involves the old confidence game or a Ponzi scheme (also common among professional criminals a hundred years ago, incidentally, when banking and cash were fairly new). The illicit often tracks the licit: When the credit markets can turn anything into a tradable security, when international currency traders try to make billions by exploiting rate discrepancies at the fourth decimal point, and when Americans of all stripes are busy trying to outfox the volatile housing market, it should come as no surprise that the netherworld wants in on the action, and senses opportunities for the more gullible among us who want some of that "easy" money, too.

Recently, I was told that my premium Yahoo! Mail account was going to renew itself if I didn't do anything about it at the cost of $20 per year. I had totally forgotten about the account, which I had set up a couple years back when I was having trouble accessing my usual e-mail account. So I clicked on the link in the e-mail message (forwarded from my Yahoo! account to my regular account). Then I got a message from Mika in Yahoo! billing asking me for personal information in order to confirm the cancellation of the account. It was late at night, and I was tired, so without another thought I dashed off an e-mail with all the digits he needed.

As I lay down and tried to fall asleep, suddenly I was struck by panic—what kind of idiot was I? I sat bolt upright in bed. I got another message by morning—this one from Omar—confirming the cancellation of my account and regretting the loss of my business. Then I noticed that the messages didn't even come from Yahoo.com. They came from "cc.yahoo-inc.com" (of course, criminals could have easily made it appear that they had come from Yahoo.com by using some sort of alias to hide the true domain of origin). My heart raced up into my throat. I clicked on that funny icon that on my e-mail program (Eudora) says "blah blah blah" to reveal the domain routing of the message. I then logged onto the IP registry to check on these folks. Eventually, I convinced myself that I had not just handed my credit card information, date of birth, password, and Social Security number over to Mika and Omar, a team of Russian and Middle Eastern Net hackers. But I still review my credit card bill a little more carefully than I used to.

As in the case of street crime, it is often children and the elderly who are the most vulnerable. My late grandmother wasn't as lucky as I was and ended up with thousands of dollars in bills, legal expenses, and creditors hounding her until she finally solved the problem by dying. Children are also relatively easier targets for both financial crime and online sexual harassment. According to the good old Pew Internet Study: "About one third (32%) of all teenagers who use the internet say they have been targets of a range of annoying and potentially menacing online activities—such as receiving threatening messages; having their private emails or text messages forwarded without consent; having an embarrassing picture posted without permission; or having rumors about them spread online."[13] And it doesn't help matters when the link for the Department of Justice's Web-based office for the Internet doesn't work.[14] Alas.

Current estimates by the FBI put the price of this type of crime at $300 billion annually. And while informational and identity crime may be on the rise, the costs of it are spread around. That's $1000 apiece; $4000 for a family of four. A lot more than my parents lost—even proportionately—when their hubcaps and television sets were stolen. That's one of the reasons—beside getting free miles and convenience—that we pay an implicit 3 percent tax on every purchase using credit cards. But it's a whole lot more pleasant being ripped off this way, sans gun, isn't it? My mother is a lot less worried about her credit card being used in the former Soviet Union (which it has been) than she was about her car window being smashed. Sure, it's a hassle, but it beats being mugged on the street, and in the end she doesn't have to pay the charges personally, even if we all do collectively. Here is an area where risk and responsibility have been spiraled upward to the collectivity—to the public commons— rather than downward to the individual (or intravidual even), where the public sphere is more robust than it was in prior eras. For everyone, that is, except the nowhere class.

Polymorphous Perversity

Family Life in the Elsewhere Society

To say the weather is hot in Tiby, Mali, is an understatement—the Sahel region that crosses Africa just below the Sahara boasts some of the highest average temperatures in the world.[1] And, not coincidentally, the people there are poor. The Fulani Tribe herd goats across the scraggly plains while their Ijaw counterparts try to grow millet, sorghum, and rice in the low-nutrient soil of the Niger Delta. Both farmers and shepherds are at the mercy of frequent droughts. Hunger abounds. Though not far in space from the famed trading city of Timbuktu at the edge of the Sahara Desert, this village is far in time from those glory days when that West African city boasted perhaps the largest library in the world and the Dogone people mapped the stars—centuries before Galileo Galilei invented the first telescope.

Mwandama, a village in Malawi—a country on the other side of the continent that many Westerners confuse with Mali on the basis that the names share all but one syllable—is equally poor. The soil is also depleted of nitrogen and other key nutrients, and the rains are unpredictable during the short growing seasons. There is little pastoral activity here. Most folks farm maize (corn) or fish the quite depleted Lake Malawi for their daily sustenance. Others go to work making mud bricks for daily wages of around 80 cents.

Other than poverty, disease, and general hardship, what do

Mali and Malawi have in common? They share the fact that both are polygamous societies. A rich Fulani herder may collect as many wives as he can afford to maintain. Ditto for the Malawan fisherman. In fact, though often officially illegal, de facto polygamy can still be found across much of the developing world (particularly in Muslim communities).

What may be shocking is that the United States has much in common with Mali and Malawi in this regard in that since the 1960s, we, too, have practiced a particular form of polygamy. All thanks to the laws of economics and human biology. For after Islamic religious status, one of the best predictors of polygamy is income inequality. And while not quite reaching the levels of inequality of African countries (yet), the United States is certainly number one in the Western world on this front.[2]

The linkage between economic inequality and polygamy is two-way—that is, polygamy both causes and is caused by inequality. High degrees of inequality tend to favor polygamy for reasons that evolutionary biologists purport to explain. Let's start with the basic fact that a man can produce thousands of offspring by spreading his seed, while a woman is physically limited to a total fertility of—at maximum—around twelve or so. But when women choose their mates, they are not just after who can provide good sperm; they also want to make sure that a would-be father both has enough resources to support a child and will, in fact, invest time and money in that child.

Confronted with a distribution of income in which the distinctions across potential suitors is not terribly great, a woman will still try to land the best catch, so to speak, but she will probably not be willing to share her man. In other words, there are a thousand other fish in the sea; so it's not really worth it to take one half (or one third, or a quarter, for that matter) of the resources of any given man (holding the distribution of genetic quality constant). Better to just go down a notch and enjoy the *complete* attention, time, and money of the next richest fellow. However, sometimes the distinctions between men are so great as to alter the calculations: If a few men control almost all of the wealth while the vast majority have very little to offer in terms of a stable source of income, then it may be worth it to be the fourth wife of the very rich man rather than the first and only wife of the poor one. You can, at least, guarantee that your babies will eat well. Of course, assuming an equal sex ratio (number of men and women in the community), for each man who enjoys the company of two wives, there is one poor sucker out there who has no conjugal relations whatsoever.

In tradition-dominated, static societies where there is a great degree of inequality and gender inequity, we can see this danger-ous dynamic emerge. There is little socioeconomic mobility for men, and there is little hope for the poorest men to reproduce. (I call it dangerous, since I can't think of a more explosive demo-graphic situation than a highly unequal, impoverished country where there is a huge contingent of frustrated, spouseless young men.)

By virtue of its rising degree of inequality, the United States has become a polygamous society as well. There are three major differences between American and African polygamy, however. The first is that ours is not a static, *Big Love*, Mormon sort of polygamy, but rather a dynamic version more appropriate to a modern society with fluid status and class positions. The second is that it is also polyandrous (i.e., multiple husbands), thanks to the income-earning potential of women. The final difference lies in the fact that dynamic polygamy is not only a reflection of inequality, it also causes inequality. In traditional polygamous societies, by contrast, polygamy often acts as a countervailing force on inequality: When a rich man procreates with many women, producing lots of offspring, it means that at the time of inheritance his formidable assets are divided among more heirs, thereby acting as an intergenerational redistribution mechanism.

What I am calling *dynamic polygamy* others may call *serial monogamy*. The difference is semantic. If "being married" means producing offspring and/or having ongoing mutual responsibilities (by virtue of those offspring or independently of them), then when you get a divorce, you are not really pressing the erase button, you are just building another thatched hut across town where you may set up with another wife while still paying child support, alimony, or plain old respects to the first. It doesn't really matter whether your second marriage started as an affair during your first; the end result from the point of view of family responsibilities is more or less the same: You have two wives (or husbands).

Contemporaneous maintenance of lovers—i.e., informal, albeit old-style, polygamy—may also be common in this era of high inequality, but unfortunately for the inquiring social scientist, real data on such arrangements are hard (if not impossible) to come by. Even if someone recorded survey responses to a question about adultery, and even if those responses seemed to vary with income inequality (or any other factor), it would be impossible to know whether the changes reflected variation in the actual prevalence of affairs or whether they merely reflected ups and downs in the tendency for individuals to honestly answer the question (which may also vary with social norms, economic circumstances, and the like). We encounter, in this regard, the same problem that criminologists face when tracking crime reports. Their imperfect solution is to focus on murder, since violently killed bodies don't often go underreported. Ours is to restrict our analysis to formal marriages.

The flip side holds, too: Many women never get to marry (or

marry very late in life) thanks to the fact that the men around them don't have the economic means to support a family. We hear the laments of many inner-city women that they would love to find a gainfully employed man to settle down with—if only one were available. In fact, in his book *The Truly Disadvantaged*, the sociologist William Julius Wilson constructs a marriageable men index (showing the ratio of women to gainfully employed, nonincarcerated men) and demonstrates that there are, on average, about sixty of these "catches" for every one hundred women in poor black neighborhoods.[3] The result is an increasing substitution among America's poor of cohabitation in lieu of formal marriage. Of course, the lack of commitment inherent in cohabitation makes dynamic polygamy all the more easy to pull off—even if it is informal in nature.

Finally, inequality is not just the cause of dynamic polygamy, it is also an effect: When a "starter" wife is left, her income drops substantially. Likewise, when some families enjoy two earners (particularly high-wage ones) and others have a single adult in residence, economic differences between those households are magnified. In fact, the largely untold story about the rise in income inequality is that family dynamics are partially to blame. Not only are those on the poor end more likely not to have two adults in the family, but when they do, they are likely to both be low-wage earners (if both are even steadily employed).[4]

Despite columnist Maureen Dowd's laments that all the rich men want to marry their secretaries, the truth is that there has been a radical realignment of marriage over the past four decades as women entered the labor force in great numbers. Successful men generally don't marry their secretaries anymore (or, for that matter, make their wives their informal career assistants post marriage); increasingly, they marry their attorneys, CPAs, or co-executives. Doctors, for example, have the highest rate of in-marriage of any profession. Yes, some high-earning women opt for the "Mommy track," but there are plenty of switches along that track. Highly educated, professional women shift back and forth between mothering and work commitments and overall work more hours than do their lower-wage counterparts (and, evidently, complain more, thanks to the greater pressure—or shadow cost—of higher wages).

Who is able to land a second spouse after a divorce is an important part of the inequality story as well. Not only do the highly paid pair up, reinforcing inequality when they are together, but the game of musical chairs more often leaves low-wage women and men standing spouseless (as it does in static monogamy). This is especially true for African Americans.[5]

Entry of women into the labor force affects the economic bargaining power of marriage partners, of course, bringing greater instability and anxiety to a previously stable, if patriarchal, institution. For example, the Negative Income Tax—a pilot program of guaranteed income support that was tested in the 1960s and '70s, and which provided women with an independent basis of economic security—actually raised the divorce rate by ostensibly providing some wives an exit route from an unhappy domestic situation.[6] The entry of women into the workforce has also been blamed by some researchers as *directly* causing higher divorce rates for the simple reason that other attractions, intimacies, and affairs are more likely to happen in gender-integrated workplaces as opposed to the time when women and men occupied very distinct social realms of home and work.

And now that work has gone global and "unplugged," so to speak, thanks to the portable workshop, all hell has broken loose. It's not just that one's exes have become more recyclable (at least in our fantasy lives) since they are now Googlable, contactable, and visitable, no matter where they live on the planet. It is also the case that with social relations delocalized, all sorts of intimacy paradoxes arise: At midnight, your ex-boyfriend, now residing overseas, instant-messages his confession that he still carries a torch for you. You glance from the glow of your laptop screen to your current sleeping boyfriend with a flash of paranoia that he saw the romantic missive before you quickly clack out your own response. Meanwhile, your best friend confesses that he is sleeping with your wife's sister, unbeknownst to his own wife. He makes you swear to tell *no one* of this, not even your wife. This intimate tie between you and your friend— replete with bonding confession and total honesty—then, paradoxically, creates a wedge in the intimacy of your own marital situation. He immediately says he regrets telling you and is sorry for putting you in such an awkward position. But he is weeping now, and rather than scolding him, you tell him that you'd rather know the truth and that his secret is safe with you (for now, at least). But as you slip into bed that evening with your wife, you are struck by the distance that has opened up between you two. Could I really tell her with little risk of it all blowing up? you wonder. Then, just as you thought you would finally be able to fall asleep, you are dogged by the question of whether she actually knows already and has just been obeying her own vow of secrecy to which her sister made her submit.

This kind of grapevine stuff has been going on at least since we lived in medieval, cobblestone villages, and probably extends as far back as the caves. What is potentially new, however, is the amount of fragmentation of our intimacies made possible by the networked Elsewhere Society. Perhaps, then, it is no surprise that the number of new homes with separate master bedroom suites is rising fast. So fast that by 2010, 60 percent of custom-built homes will have them, according to the *New York Times*. (Perhaps the final step is the development of multiple bedrooms for each person, so that when the various aspects of his/her self are tired s/he can sleep in the appropriate room, moving around from bed to bed as each fragment asserts its control.)

We have come full circle: At one time we lived in tribes. These devolved into extended kin networks (living with the cousins, and grandma, too). That was replaced by the nuclear family. But then this unit also broke down—or, rather, *devolved,* to use a less judgmental term. Now we circulate like electron clouds through the networks of love and human connection. So perhaps it is ironic that in our supermodern—or postmodern— Elsewhere Society, intraviduals end up with love networks that look a lot like those of African villagers.

The irony of this system lies in the fact that women who focus their efforts on landing a man and becoming housewives tend to suffer from the most turmoil in their domestic lives and live at the mercy of an unequal labor market and fickle men, according to the sociologist Susan Thistle, whose book *From Marriage to the Market* tracked the lives of postfeminist women.[7] By contrast, those who manage to lay the groundwork for economic independence—by getting more education and diving into the work of work—are the ones who end up with the most stable and fulfilling marriages. After all, it is not just women who are selecting mates based on their provider potential. As women have now become serious breadwinners (and are better educated than men, on average), men may face the same incentive structures when picking their mates as women do (Dowd's complaints notwithstanding).

NO KID-DING AROUND

For this realignment of marriage to occur, it was not just women's labor force participation and education levels that needed to change. Nor were advances in telecommunications technologies enough. Demographic shifts were required as well. Specifically, the number of children we have has dropped by half on average (and even more in European countries) in the fifty years since Mrs. 1959 was raising her brood. Of course, this has paved the way for mothers (and fathers) to have entries, exits, and re-entries to the labor market as their children require, at first, a lot of care, and then progressively less as they move into the school system. Back in the days of five or six kids, there was almost always a little one around who needed tending to.

These changes in fertility have not only affected the home-work balance but have also changed the very way that we view and raise those same kids themselves. The laws of economics tell us that when there is fewer of something, it is more valuable. So our children have perhaps become more precious (think diamonds). This effect is probably redoubled by the fact that we wait longer to get them—the average age at first birth has been rising steadily from 21.5 in 1960 to 25.2 today.[8] (Kids can tell you that the longer they have to suffer a wait for something, the more they value it.) Though our own parents may deny that they treasured us any less, any casual observation of the children of professional parents today would suggest that they are treated like rare specimens, freaks of nature even, who rarely enjoy a minute unsupervised by an adult. Of course, the need for adult labor to supervise our children fits quite nicely into the service sector pyramid: Well-paid professionals need to hire not-so-well compensated child care workers to shuttle their kids to and from soccer leagues and Mandarin lessons while they take meetings back at the (n)office or the café.

The streets are safer than ever, yet we don't let our kids outside to play. (Or perhaps they are safer *because* we don't let our kids out.) They are too busy. The frequency of structured after-school activities has more than doubled over the last two decades for the average American kid.[9] Likewise, homework has been creeping down the grade ladder so far that even many kindergartners have to stress out about getting their assignments in on time. All this happens despite substantial evidence that neither homework quantity nor quality in early grades predicts achievement later on, when it matters.[10] Such research misses the point, however: Homework serves to train the still plastic brains of our children to get used to constantly elevated levels of cortisol (a stress hormone)—that is, we are getting them accustomed to the feeling of falling behind in their paperwork. After all, each economic system must socialize its children to fit its ethic. Why should education be any different today than during the heyday of the industrial era, when elite children were taught managerial skills and the working-class kids were taught to sit still and do as they are told by their superiors?

To reward our hard little worker, we don't give our child a doll per se; rather, we give her a "Webkin," which is, yes, technically a doll of sorts, but the far more popular part of the package is the doll's identity online. In a reversal of the symbolic and the real, the physical *thing* (made in China) merely serves as the "real-world" avatar of the online identity of the horsie, platypus, or other synthetic creature that we have purchased. Our kids understand this right away, even if we don't. They just chuck aside the polypropylene-filled doll into the corner of their room and run to log on to the network with the secret code that comes attached to the collar so they can initiate their new pet's account. These young users of "Webkinz.com" grew in number from 1 million in 2006 to 6 million in 2007 (though by the time you are reading this, there may be a newer, hotter site).[11] And what do they do the moment this creature has been activated? They get busy merging work and leisure just like mom and dad do. They do mazes, quizzes, and other knowledge games to earn points or coins.

It's not just knowledge work, though. In case some kids are destined for the expansive, low-wage food service industry, they can find work on the internationally popular Club Penguin site, which has more than doubled its traffic from 1.9 million users to almost 5 million in one year. There's always a place on the assembly line making pizzas for the flightless birds (anchovy, of course). This sustenance is not fed directly to the kid's own penguin (nor to that penguin's pet "puffle") but rather earns them money in the playful economy, so they can purchase food for their dependents in a perfect mimicry of the way we parents have outsourced basic survival tasks to the global marketplace. And global it is: Club Penguin allows you to log on to any server you like, enabling the free market to balance the traffic across sites such as Outback, Yukon, or Iceland. These and many other servers are purportedly located across much of the English-speaking commonwealth in the United Kingdom, Canada, the United States, and Australia. Who knows? They are probably in a closet somewhere in Hyderabad, India, but the kids certainly sort themselves by national grouping, perhaps thinking the server response will be quicker the nearer the headquarters is to their own location.

Of course, social science research coincidentally—if not magically—confirms that what middle- and upper-class folks do with their kids is the right thing (even if we do let them use the computer a little too much, that online weisure is only a reward for finishing their math homework, scoring a goal at soccer, or doing their extracurricular piano practice). Annette Lareau shows this in her book *Unequal Childhoods:* Outside of school, the time spent by well-off and poor kids could not be more different. Poor children spend 40 percent more time in unstructured activities than middle-class kids. Whereas the middle class has signed their kids up for ever more soccer leagues, music lessons, and myriad other after-school activities, the poor do not have that luxury.[12] Their kids, disproportionately, spend time "hanging out"; this has also been observed by Jason DeParle in his chronicle of three welfare families struggling through the era of reform in Milwaukee, *American Dream*.[13]

· The results of these differences in how they spend their time, according to sociologists and psychologists, is that middle- and upper-class kids know how to follow abstract rules, are more cognitively stimulated, and are used to dealing with non-kin adults—particularly authority figures—in a way that is more equal (i.e., they have reasoned arguments with their soccer coaches while poor kids disproportionately get yelled at to "fall in line" with a constantly looming threat of punishment). The middle-class kids also benefit from the skills and confidence instilled during these organized activities. The poor, by contrast, are more often left to a *Lord of the Flies* existence in a child-dominated world separated from the vocabulary-expanding world of adults. In fact, this class fault line through the lives of children is reflected in research about mothers' time with their kids.

The early childhood sociologist Amy Hsin, for example, finds that each additional hour a highly educated mother spends with her children benefits their subsequent scores on cognitive tests and behavioral measures. The catch is that such "quality time" is only good if the mom herself scores high on such tests. If she is a less educated mother with a smaller vocabulary, there is no impact one way or another on her kids of their time spent together. She might as well neglect them—at least according to the rational economics of the family.[14]

This study opens a window into the dirty little (politically incorrect) secret of the much ballyhooed "Mommy wars," which debate the impact of mom's staying home versus various forms of day care on the outcomes of children of various ages. It seems—at first glance—that the studies on whether it is better to care for children at home as opposed to formal day care or preschool come to a mishmash of conflicting results. But upon closer examination, a very clear pattern emerges from the voluminous research literature now out there: While, of course, the quality of day care matters with respect to its impact on kids, what is equally, if not more, important is the "quality" of the mother. The kids of well-educated, middle-class moms suffer worse outcomes when they are separated from their mothers early in life (put into day care or preschool). By contrast, young children in poor families actually do *better* in terms of standard cognitive and behavioral measures when they spend more time in formal day care settings (such as the Head Start program) and less time being taken care of by their biological mothers.[15]

Linking the time-use studies with the day care ones suggests that what lower-class and upper-class kids are doing when they are at home is radically divergent. The typical poor kid is probably sitting in front of the television for hours. Even when professional-class and working-class kids are both just staring at a monitor screen, what they are looking at tends to be different. Thanks to much higher rates of broadband access, upper-income kids are more likely to be playing the Webkinz sort of knowledge games or logging onto multiuser domains (MUDs) that have a significant text-based component to their interactivity.[16] Poorer kids tend to play a Nintendo handheld or other system that involves pressing buttons and shooting things. Again, never let it be said that society isn't good at somehow subtly structuring every minute of our kids' time to put them in their respective places, so to speak.

For a while, researchers tried to nail down exactly what the key differences were—that magic bullet for getting your kid into Harvard. Was it time spent reading together? That turned out to be a canard. After all, going on a hike may be just as important or interactive than reading (and even more Socratic). The next measure pursued was number of words spoken per hour. More educated folk tended to run their mouths more, it turned out. A lot more. Was it active or passive activity that was key (direct social engagement v. just hanging out)? Hsin's study showed that it didn't really matter what the mom and kid were doing—if the parent had a big vocabulary, then they might as well be smoking crack together and the kid would still get a bump in his SATs. Apparently, highly educated parents have a *je ne sais quoi* that seeps into their kids.

The stakes for parents are high—kids, after all, reflect our class status more than any other marker. According to Mitchell Stevens, author of *Creating a Class: College Admissions and the Education of Elites,* you can have a fancy car, house, and a high-powered job, but if you fail to get your kids into an elite college, then you have ultimately failed in your status attainment efforts. And all your material success suffers from the immoral tinge of being a bad parent.[17] No, it's not enough to be head of the company; you have to be that *and* show the world that you have invested enough hours at home that your kids get into Princeton. Too bad those pesky little buggers don't always go along with the plan.

It is only in this climate that *The Dangerous Book for Boys* becomes an ironic best seller. (Ironic in that it begs the question, How dangerous can a *manual* for fun be?) A whole new slew of books tell us that we have overprogrammed our children. Let kids be kids, they tell us. Just as quickly they add that children, these days, don't have enough creative time for imaginative play. We are stunting their creative growth by scheduling them so much. And, of course, the new elite wants to fashion their offspring into visionary thinkers to lead Richard Florida's Creative

Class. But parents respond ambivalently: It is a high-risk strat-egy, after all, to just let your kids do what they please and hope that your supersmart genes shine through—especially in an era with so many "lowbrow" temptations all around us.

Some parents try to solve both problems—the potential of overscheduling to kill creativity and the temptations of brain-numbing diversions—in one fell swoop by subscribing to the Waldorf approach to schooling, which bans plastic toys, televi-sion, fast food, and the rest of popular culture in an effort to pro-tect young ones so that their minds can develop naturally and purely.[18] The irony in this anti-structure backlash movement is that lying just underneath all the rhetoric about "allowing kids just to be kids" is the argument that we are going to do this so that they will be stronger, faster, smarter, better (when it comes time to apply to college, of course). It's the same motivation, just a difference in strategy. The Waldorfians and their kin are trying to effect the Tortoise to the super-soccer mom's Hare, but they are competing in the same achievement decathlon nonetheless.

The Birth of the Intravidual

All along I have been describing how modern boundaries that we once took for granted have given way, crumbling under the force of family, economic, and technological change. Perhaps the most fundamental line that has been breached is that between the "self" and the "other." The interpenetration of the social world into our daily consciousness—our orientation to elsewhere—has the ultimate effect of colonizing and fragmenting not just our attentions but our very identities. The result is often a competing cacophony of multiple selves all jostling for pole position in our mind.

These resulting intraviduals whom I have alluded to throughout this book are the various horcruxes—to borrow the language of *Harry Potter*—that together would theoretically make a complete self. I try to imply the fragmentation of the individual by instead using the prefix *intra*, meaning "within." The irony, of course, is that the intravidual is just as much an "intervidual" (*inter* meaning "between"), since it is the networked nature of our new, Elsewhere economy and the penetration of others into us that shatters the individual.[1]

When you grow up in a divorced family, shuttling between two houses, you know instinctively (if that were not an oxymoron in this context) that you are really two (or more) different people: one with your mom during the week and the other on weekends with your dad. If you speak two languages, you know that you can literally have two different personalities in the respective countries or cultures. Traders and other such figures have long occupied niches between communities and have even spanned entire societies. But today we can *all* occupy that ambivalent position to group society that Georg Simmel called "the stranger" a hundred years ago.

Before the intravidual could come about in social history, however, the individual had to arrive on the scene. With the movement of large masses of people to cities, the undifferentiated mass of collective consciousness was said to have begun to fragment. Encountering many strangers—different folks from many walks of life—the urban resident encountered a hitherto unknown freedom. This is when, supposedly, we learned to think for ourselves, becoming modern individuals. But many urban sociologists believe that there was a price to pay for this in the form of a blasé attitude among city dwellers. Such an attitude was necessary to protect the self from the constant stimulation of fast-paced urban life. While disaffected, the city dweller was not disconnected. In fact, this new individualism, paradoxically, results from groups.

According to Georg Simmel, premodern society (what used to be known as primitive society) is characterized by concentric group affiliations. That means that everyone in my family lives in my village; everyone in my village lives under the same king; everyone in the kingdom shares the same ethnicity, religion, and so on and so forth. Russian nesting dolls provide an adequate metaphor. By contrast, modern society is characterized by sets of overlapping affiliations that may be unique to each person. Our town and our family may not coincide, for example, if our sister has moved to another state. Nor might our nation and our religion, if we happen to be part of a minority group that got "trapped" in a state that was founded on a single religion model.

(Think Iranian Jews, for example.) In fact, not everyone in a given family may even share citizenship (my kids are Australian even though I am American). If any one of us were to list all of our affiliations, we'd probably find out that we are unique: voilà—the birth of the individual. Through membership in many disparate groups, we become individuated. This individualism was supposedly born sometime around 1789, in Paris, and was blamed for the disintegration of French society in the wake of the ancien régime. In the English-speaking world, the term didn't come into usage until 1835, but certainly the underlying concept was present right through the Scottish Enlightenment.

Recently, something has changed about this traditional formula: Namely, the networked economy and society has made us intraviduals by breaking down physical barriers to group affiliation. In the modern city, the individual emerged from these overlapping affiliations, which were located in a unitary social place: the person. All interaction had to take place face-to-face. As such, while membership in a guild or a religious order may have linked the person to a wider, "imagined community," that larger group was always beyond the social horizon. What made up social interaction, and thus identity, was the interaction with the local representatives of the various larger groups to which I nominally belonged: Interacting in my apartment block, I meet my Catholic neighbor; at the office, I encounter a Scottish colleague, and our conversation makes me acutely aware of being American; at the green market in Union Square I meet farmers from rural Vermont, who make me self-conscious about being a jaded New Yorker; and of course, I never feel my race as acutely as when I enter a predominantly black church on a Sunday. The sum total of these—as well as many other—experiences creates my uniqueness as an individual.

The creation of the individual self in this process was a

two-way street. I choose to affiliate with certain groups: my professional society, perhaps; my church; the PTA at my children's school; my bowling league; and so on. But to the extent that those groups are pervasive—everyone I know belongs to them—they do little to distinguish me as an individual (for example, someone may live in a city that is all Muslim, and thus while her own Islamic identity may play a big part in her life, it obviously does not make her unique). Similarly, if there is difference in a given community—for example, there are Protestants and Catholics; whites and non-whites; managers and workers; Republicans and Democrats—but if all the proverbial sticks fall on either side of some symbolic line, then this fails to create individuals as well. In other words, if all the Protestants are white Republican managers and all the Catholics are non-white Democratic workers, then the collective consciousness is probably pretty strong and individualism does not emerge.

It is only when the groups don't match up—when we are confronted with difference and when those differences are multifaceted—that the individual emerges. In this way, it is not a choice. It's not all about voluntary association. It's also about differences that are noted by others about us. We may feel like a woman inside, for example, but look like a man to everyone else—to take the case of gender. These disjunctures mean that we need to see ourselves as others see us in our social calculations—something that every kid learns to do, with the notable exception of many children on the autistic spectrum. Self-reflectiveness—and thus individualism and the social self—arises from creating an *objective* view of ourselves when we are forced into the exercise of seeing us as others who don't share our identities see us.

The number of affiliations I could have was generally limited by the demands of face time. Slowly, however, modern telecommunications have eroded that looking-glass aspect of confronting the other in the modern metropolis. We can now belong to—affiliate with—groups with which we have little physical contact and/or lack any common organizing theme or totem. In premodern society, the groups to which we belonged were not only concentrically organized, they were also ascriptive—that is, based on conditions of birth over which we had little control. We were born into a certain ethnic group, a certain religion, a certain feudal estate or social caste. These groups penetrated every aspect of our lives and consciousnesses. And, for the most part, we had little choice about those group memberships; we could not change them any more than we could change our physical bodies. In modern society, group membership shifted to include many seemingly voluntary associations. We ostensibly choose our church, our occupation, our place of residence, our spouse (as compared to the arranged marriages that dominated the prior epoch), and our bowling league. Of course, we still live with many ascriptive identities—hence the continued power of race and gender in the United States.

In positing that the modern individual came from the unique intersection of affiliations with myriad groups, Simmel faces a paradox of sorts. What is driving the selection of group memberships if not a preexisting individual with preferences? But where do preferences come from if not from the socialization of groups? Of course, there must be some preexisting self that throws off the chains of ascription. Hence, the phrase, "finding oneself"—the modern imperative to discover the natural or biological tendencies and preferences and to fashion our social world (our choice of partner, of job, of place to live, and so on) so that it is in accordance with the supposed underlying natural (and whole) self.

In the postmodern or information economy, those restraints

have been totally removed. You can join as many groups as you want, deploying multiple aliases while you are at it. Members of stigmatized groups have always experienced the phenomenon of multiple selves: macho black men who seek gay sex on the down low, for instance; Communists during the McCarthy era; or even politicians today who happen to be atheists but dare not admit it. The difference is that today there is no need for *anyone* to reconcile the many facets of their identities. They can just create a new e-mail account for that gay affair, that membership in the online Wicca group, or that Dungeons & Dragons user group that the CEO finds too embarrassing to own up to in the presence of work colleagues.

Ever since the time of de Tocqueville, America has been known as a land of "joiners." What we lacked in voter turnout, we made up for in our rich civic life. Americans attended more meetings of voluntary associations than did any other population on the planet. However, something interesting has happened as of late: We are joining more but participating less, in the words of the Harvard political scientist Theda Skocpol.[2] We still have higher rates of affiliation than any other nation (in fact, higher than ever), but we now typically write checks or click on a Web site rather than get together and spend our precious time. And in some cases, it isn't really possible to "get together." The Internet has allowed for all sorts of geographically dispersed associations based on common interests or characteristics—the National Association of Left-Handed Golfers is just one example.

At least all of the above examples are social affiliations that have some content. The irony of the online social networking craze is that Web 2.0 sites like Orkut, Friendster, Facebook, and MySpace are all group and no beef. The broader the networks reach—and many of these try to connect the whole world—

the less meaningful they necessarily have to be. That's because content = exclusivity.

Now when we log on to Facebook, we see not just our friends, but who our friends' friends are, and which networks are most common among them. We can then ask to be friends with those folks, too. On the lower-brow MySpace, we don't even need to be friends—that is, approved by someone—for us to go nosing around their social network or personal profile. And we can ask total strangers to be our buddies with little more to go on than how they look and what answers they've plugged into a series of prescripted questions intended to reveal their inner world. While there remains the possibility of being rejected as a "friend," blocked by a user, or even taken down off the site by the administrator if s/he deems your content offensive, for the most part the boundaries of social groups on these online networks has become so diluted as to lose all exclusivity. And with no exclusivity, there is no meaning to the group. No meaning to the group, then no identity. No identity, then no self. We can look at everyone, but we see right through them to their own "friends," and so on, ad infinitum, in a hall of one-way social mirrors.

At the same time, this new, networked economy erodes any sense of the private—all in the name of being connected. Netflix is the largest online movie distributor. Like Amazon.com for books, it provides recommendations to users based on past transactions. But Netflix goes beyond Amazon in allowing—in fact, encouraging—users to rate as many films as possible in order to get a sense of one's preferences. These preferences are then used to filter recommendations. They may be based on directors, genres, or actors you seem to prefer. But the newest aspect of the system is the use of social networks in the recommendation process. Specifically, my recommendations arise primarily from the list of movies I haven't seen but which others, who tend to like what I have also rated highly, have seen and enjoyed. There are, of course, adjustments for individuals' tendencies to be tough or easy critics, for the degree of overlap, for the variation in preferences, and so on. The core of the system, however, remains the notion that I will like what others who have similar tastes have recommended.

Sometimes this system works extremely well. The other night, my children and I watched what my Netflix compatriots thought would be a wonderful film—*Ring of Bright Water*—about a man who adopts an otter as his pet and as a result quits the hustle and bustle of London for the quiet life of coastal Scotland. Had I trekked down to my local video store, there is no doubt that they would not have carried this obscure movie due to limited shelf space. Not only would my local video store not have been able to afford the shelf space to stock *Ring of Bright Water*, but the issue more germane to the present discussion is that I would have never even known to ask for it. In fact, short of some chance encounter of a recommendation at a dinner party, I would have never even known that this 1969 British film existed. The fact that I now know it exists can be attributed to the network basis of the Netflix recommendation system.

The connected economy, then, does not merely facilitate sameness and the diffusion of hits. It can encourage niche consumption (as Chris Anderson celebrates in *The Long Tail*). But as wonderful as it is to have a computer recommend a sleeper film that even the slacker clerks at my neighborhood video store wouldn't be able to name, there is a subtle cost to this form of knowledge diffusion. If Amazon had told me that "other white men between ages 35 and 45" also bought Ian McEwan's latest novel and Joan Didion's memoir, I might find it offensive. As modernists, we don't take well to the salience of ascriptive categories. They feel reductive and demeaning of our individuality. If Amazon instead said, "Professors and social scientists who enjoy travel and live in urbanized settings" also enjoyed *The End of Poverty* by Jeffrey Sachs, then we might find it a little strange as well, even though it's based on my achieved—or affiliational—characteristics. We may bristle at being reduced to a half-dozen cultural, occupational, or lifestyle characteristics, as the character Allison does in *Annie Hall* when Alvy Singer (Woody Allen's role) says: "You, you, you're like New York, Jewish, left-wing, liberal, intellectual, Central Park West, Brandeis University, the socialist summer camps and the, the father with the Ben Shahn drawings, right, and the really, y'know, strike-oriented kind of, red diaper, stop me before I make a complete imbecile of myself."

"No," she replies sarcastically, "that was wonderful. I love being reduced to a cultural stereotype."

Simmel claimed, after all, that our individuality comes from the unique intersection of groups that we embody. When it doesn't feel so unique anymore—thanks to Amazon or Woody Allen—our very selfhood is diminished.

Yet when Amazon tells us that we might also enjoy the *Captain Underpants* series since we just purchased another children's graphic novel that was bought, in turn, by folks who got *Captain Underpants,* we say thanks. But this is just as powerful a form of social assignment. (Why not offer random selections from the millions of books or DVDs in the library?) And while not making social connections based on explicit identities, the computer applets are reducing the complexity of near-infinite choice by creating implicitly defined groups. In many ways such network-based categorizations are more insidious that the hackneyed groupings based on race, class, gender, religion, or any other demographic characteristic: The rules of assignment are not made explicit; there is no totem; and the group is, in fact, a group-less group.

This first point is fairly straightforward: Although the programmers in Palo Alto *may* know the formulas that go into the recommendation process, we certainly don't.* In fact, the Amazon (or Google pagerank) formula may even be beyond the knowledge of any single programmer in the same way that a modern, industrial machine such as the automobile is too complicated for any single line worker or engineer to fathom in its entirety.

Second, there is no totem to these groups. Ironically, by tailoring our consumer choices so narrowly to our previous preferences (as they align with the preferences of others), we create a situation of a group of one—myself—in which my uniqueness fails to create an individual because it is not created from the overlap of meaningful groups of "others" but rather from a formula based on purchases recommending purchases. Like looking up a word in the dictionary and then the words in that definition and so on, it ultimately yields a self-referential loop unanchored to anything else.

Users often strike back, of course, creating common interest groups on the Internet. This is, essentially, an effort to upload a modernist, offline notion of the group onto the social network platform in much the same way one might import a bunch of songs from a physical CD into an iTunes library. In this way, the modern and postmodern can peacefully commingle. Yet

---

*Much the same issue is at work in the construction of what is arguably the most important number in your life: your credit score. Credit scores are calculated based on a proprietary equation that is unknown not only to the rated but also to many of the consumers of the output such as banks and credit card companies. What's more, they have been shown to be poor and biased predictors of actual loan repayment capability.

sometimes when these two distinct forms of social interaction are merged together, the result is not pretty. I agreed to list my co-worker—who I obviously know in a meaningful offline context—as a friend on Netflix. As in almost any networked site, the choice had to be mutual. Once we had both agreed, however, we then had full access to each other's movie-viewing activity. I knew which films she was currently watching; she, in turn, knew which were on my list. The ostensible benefits of being able to take and make recommendations from a trusted (offline) friend were more than outweighed by the icky sense that my private viewing habits had been made a matter of semi-public concern (even though I hadn't even been nominated to the Supreme Court).

But I was bringing a modernist conception of privacy to the online world. Privacy as we knew it was predicated on a certain division between "front stage" and "back stage" (to use the phrases of the sociologist Erving Goffman). The front stage is where we present ourselves according to a certain script and where everyone knows and expects social life to follow a patterned structure. Back stage, in short, is where we can be ourselves, where we may let others peek in once in a while to see the "real" us—the authentic self. However, in a world where identities are not anchored within a single body—at the intersection of those group affiliations—there is no "authenticity" to act as lodestone for a private self. When we can have multiple selves with the click of a mouse and the creation of a new online identity, there is no single core to protect from public view. Self-protection is not achieved by withholding; rather, it is accomplished by offering up more and more information and identities until each identity is everywhere in the social house of mirrors and we cannot know from "authentic" anymore. We hide in plain sight.

Thus, the quintessential group of our epoch is not the Sikh student association that happens to maintain an online presence; rather, it is the ungroup, the Escher-like social network that is finite, yet boundless (as is our view of the universe itself). We have gone from the rigid, embedded group memberships of pre-modern societies, to the affiliational ones of the modern individual, to the porous, nominal ungroups of the current age. There are no boundaries. If you click on one of the books that Amazon recommended to you when you bought this one, then you are connected to yet another group of books to which that book belonged, perhaps ad infinitum. (I personally have never hit a dead end or gotten trapped in a loop when I have followed the hyperlinks of Amazon recommendations.)

In this way, the book is now the node in the network and the invisible user (or purchaser) is now the tie between objects. The collection of monetary interest was seen as immoral by the medieval Church, since the creation of money through lending it to another individual subjugated that individual to the money by making the social relationship between bank accounts and the individual the mere link between past and future amounts. (Islam still forbids the charging of interest on loans.) Had Face-book or Amazon existed back then, perhaps they would have been outlawed as well, since now the person is just the tie to another set of individuals (in the case of MySpace) or another collection of objects (in the case of Netflix).

The result for the user is the relational equivalent of the BlackBerry-induced Elsewhere Society: social relations for the sake of gaining additional social relations. Knowing people for the sake of who they connect us to. When I was a freshman in college at Berkeley, I was stunned by how students interacted with each other on Sproul Plaza—the main drag on campus. First of all, almost everyone wore sunglasses. I suppose this was to be expected in California, where the sun literally appeared to shine more brightly than it did back East—bouncing off shiny, metallic objects with an almost piercing glare. Still, for a New Yorker accustomed to intense eye contact, it was certainly disconcerting to be in a place where I couldn't tell whether or not the person was looking at me. Soon, however, I discovered that I could occasionally see through the Rayban wraparounds. My interlocutors were not, in fact, looking at me as they conversed. They were looking elsewhere. Further observation revealed that I should not have necessarily taken it personally: When almost everyone interacted with everyone else, they were looking askance, as in the famous Renoir painting *The Boating Party*. There might be a more enticing social encounter just beyond the corner of one's eye, so better to keep scanning, like a social searchlight.

This feeding frenzy for more and more social connections is driven by the sociological and business books that tell us that it's not what you know, it's who you know. The theory is actually based on solid, if outdated, research. Back in 1967, Stanley Milgram, an American psychologist, set up an experiment to test an idea that had been circulating for a while, namely, that every individual could be connected to another individual through a relatively small number of mutual acquaintances. Milgram recruited participants in Omaha, Nebraska, and gave them a letter that they were instructed to give, by hand, to someone they knew (either directly or a "friend of a friend"). The goal was to get the letter to a stockbroker in Sharon, Massachusetts, 1,452 miles away.[3] The results of this experiment formed the basis of our common-day notion of "six degrees of separation"—the idea that any two people in the world can be connected through only six people (at most). (Research on this theory has continued, and it looks like the true number of links is probably closer to eight or nine.) If not quite marking the birth of the coming network society, certainly Milgram's experiment inaugurated the science of networks that would be needed to study such a hyperlinked society. Although the experiment had actually been preceded by much network research during the 1950s and even earlier, the Milgram study gave us one of the two tropes or ethics that have come to dominate the network society: The notion of small worlds that are totally interconnected. More recent work by sociologist Duncan Watts has refined the "small world" hypothesis, finding that it works because particular individuals act as connectors across huge swaths of social (and geographical) space, thereby making social networks "scale free."

That is all well and nice, but the clincher came a few years after the original Milgram study, in 1972, when another sociologist, Mark Granovetter, gave us the second ethic of the network society in an article that would become a classic in social science and beyond. In "The Strength of Weak Ties," Granovetter argued that, ironically, it is often relatively *weak ties*—connections to folks you don't know all that well and that are not reinforced by other indirect pathways—that turn out to be quite valuable because they bring new information. The strength of weak ties has been found to be especially useful for job (and romantic) searches. In a densely connected network, all the individuals probably know the same people, hear of the same job openings, have the same contacts, and so on. By contrast, your next-door neighbor from childhood, whom you only see once in a while when you go home to visit your parents and aren't close friends with but think is generally a nice person, probably has a completely different set of connections. The irony is that this weak tie provides the most opportunities.[4]

For his landmark study, Granovetter interviewed professionals in Boston. He discovered that among his fifty-four respondents who found their employment via personal network ties, more than half saw this contact "occasionally" (less than once a week but more than once a year). Perhaps even more surprising was the fact that the runner-up to this category was not folks who the responders saw "often" (once a week or more); it was those they saw "rarely" (once a year or less) by a factor of almost 2 to 1. All of a sudden deep human relationships are found wanting; the real payoff is in knowing lots of folks who don't know one another. Perhaps, then, it is no longer rude *not* to introduce your friends to each other. Each "structural hole" (gap between people or groups) in our personal social network is worth money and power. It's a simple law of arbitrage: The more information that has to flow through you—since there are no other pathways for it to get from one part of the network to the other—the more you can profit from the information gap. This is what traders do, essentially, and real estate brokers (who try to create a gap through exclusive agreements).

In the networked economy, however, we face a paradox of small worlds and weak ties. It is the increased interconnectedness that makes a single bound from Peoria to Manila possible. But it is the easy connecting nature of the Internet that makes those structural holes (and the accompanying social power) all the more difficult to hold on to, since it is quite easy to Google someone ourselves. As it turns out, in certain circumstances weak ties aren't all that they're cracked up to be. According to recent research by sociologist Damon Centola, when we want to change our behavior in ways that aren't so easy—say, go on a diet, learn calculus, or train for a marathon—it is the strong ties that matter. Better to go to WeightWatchers with your lifelong friends. Better study for the SATs with the other soldiers from your foxhole. And better kick heroin with your drug gang. Behavioral messages that work the best are those that come from folks we know deeply and whose relationship to us is reinforced through many indirect ties.[5] Hence the concept of the intervention, where all that strong social capital is brought to bear on a deviant individual (alcoholic, drug addict, compulsive shoplifter) in one hard blow.

But an economy that favors movement and motion, one that needs weak ties to reach faraway markets in distant lands, a service economy where our customers, clients, and colleagues (not to mention investors) are drawn from the electronic Rolodex—this is an economy that favors the weak tie over the strong one. So we go from tribes, where we have little control over whom we interact with and where our identity stems from ascriptive affiliations that are matters of luck, to modern mobile families, where individuals are born through the unique intersections of their chosen (achieved) group affiliations, to globalized, amorphous clouds of network nodes (ungroups) on Facebook, where how we know someone is trivial compared to the fact that we do know them. In the process, however, we somehow have managed to lose our selves. Maybe the key moment was when we stopped looking at each other in the eye. Or maybe it happened the first time that someone created a second e-mail account. Or maybe it occurred when Google trumped the sorting of Web pages by content with its site rankings by number of referring links.

Conclusion

Learning to Love the BlackBerry

I recently went to see my favorite professional football team, the New York Giants, play against one of their bitter rivals from just down the road, the Philadelphia Eagles. I have been going to the football games on and off with my father for much of my life. Lately, however, it's been more difficult for me to go. Difficult in two senses. First, while my mother accepted that football was like another spouse with whom she had to share her husband, my own wife brooks no such deal. I am expected to—and do—play a major role in raising our children, so taking a Sunday off to go watch grown men smash into each other in "a meaningless game" (her words, obviously) is not high on the "family's" priority list. We both travel a lot for work, too, and that generally takes precedence over a trip to the stadium.

Perhaps if I brought my son or daughter along, I could combine the child care with the football. But the problem is that they have basically no interest in professional football (or other spectator sports, for that matter). When I was eight, I saved up for baseball or football cards to collect and trade with my friends. My children, by contrast, prefer Pokemon cards. The concept is not much different—each card lists a series of stats that can be memorized by obsessed children. Kids trade their doubles or multiple weaker cards for a single strong one. But rather than representing a sports hero, the cards they clutch in their sweaty palms are physical avatars of make-believe online creatures with names like Squirtle, Charmander, Mewtwo, and, most famously, Pikachu. Like football merchandising, there are not just cards to collect, there are movies to watch, video games to play, stuffed animals to amass, and so on.

So the whole experience at Giants Stadium is tinged with parental guilt as well as the bitterness of the strife I will have to endure from my wife upon my return home. (I suppose she is little different from most football widows in this respect.) But there are aspects of the game-day experience that have changed as well. Advertisements have pervaded every inch of the stadium. Bottled water is sold for five dollars a pop even though the drinking fountains work. (You can't bring any bottles—even plastic ones—into the stadium; the Giants corporation relied on security measures post 9/11 to increase its monopoly power for the concession stands.) And the price of tickets has risen so steeply that more and more professionals attend what was once the almost exclusive domain of working-class men. There are more and more women in the stands, as well.

Not satisfied with these rising revenues, the stadium has added luxury boxes where corporate executives can show potential clients a good time on a Sunday afternoon that might have been family time in years past. The Giants can charge a small fortune for these lavish vestibules since the companies write them off as business expenses for tax purposes—not to mention the fact that the managers who make the decisions to purchase a box are generally so far removed from the shareholders as to not really be accountable as to whether they are *worth* the expense. Recently, the Giants have decided that—given their long waiting list for tickets and their desire to sell more of these high revenue corporate boxes—the current stadium is not big enough. So, next to the existing Giants Stadium, a new one is being constructed, partially funded by taxpayer dollars. Even as every game is sold out, the owners perhaps keep an excited eye peeled eastward to the skeleton of the new arena that plugs along, estimated to be completed by 2011. Given the sold-out status of all the games, scalped tickets are as common as they have ever been; however, rather than issuing warnings about the illegality of buying scalped tickets, now the Giants facilitate such exchanges by providing an online marketplace. These online auctions work in practice since the important part of the ticket for gate entry is the bar code and I.D. number that can be printed out from any computer.

The new breed of fan behaves differently at the game, too. Rather than flasks of whiskey, many now bring cell phones and call friends or family to offer a play-by-play account, or relay something others may have missed by watching the game on TV. Others are text-messaging. In fact, the stadium runs a Verizon-sponsored text-messaging trivia contest which, once you play it a single time, locks you into receiving Giants text messages (at, perhaps, five cents a pop, depending on your plan) from Verizon over the course of the entire season unless you take the time and effort to turn it off by finding and logging onto a Web site. I am one of these multitasking, professional, distracted fans and have trouble putting my e-mail- and text-message-equipped cell phone away to focus attention on the game we just paid a fortune to attend.

But some things about the stadium experience have not changed over the decades. Despite efforts to reduce postgame DUI by restricting beer sales to the first half, many folks end up drunk and rowdy. Fights break out; some folks strip off their shirts in freezing cold weather; and despite the piped-in music (the same tunes for most teams across America), tried-and-true team chants emerge spontaneously from the crowd ("Here we go, Giants, here we go!" or, "Deee-fence; Deee-fence"). And then there is the mugging for the TV cameras. During breaks, the cameras sometimes turn toward the crowd. What usually ensues is a shot on the scoreboard of a group of fans jumping wildly up and down, perhaps one or more of them waving a huge foam finger in the air. The thing is, though, they are for the most part *not* looking into the camera. Instead, they are watching themselves on the big screen, which means the camera angle catches their profiles and lots of shots of folks pointing to the images of themselves overhead. Many people quickly discover this, and then turn toward the camera. And yet, most of these folks still can't resist the temptation to turn back to the screen images of themselves.

Who can blame them? They are caught in the Catch-22 of our linked-in society. If they wave (and look) at the camera, it makes for a better shot—the whole stadium can see them for their five seconds of fame. But in that case, they themselves miss out on the experience totally. After all, most of the time these shots are not being broadcast on TV, so there is no hope of TiVo-ing the moment. They are just closed-circuited to the 76,000 or so fans who are there with them. If, however, those lucky fans watch themselves, in order to fully take in the experience of having one's likeness splayed across a hundred-foot monitor in view of tens of thousands of folks, then they've ruined it, since their faces are obscured.

This video Catch-22 (not to mention the entire scene of the hyperconsumerist football stadium with its own replacement being constructed a few hundred feet away) is a metaphor for the paradoxical choices American intraviduals often face in today's Elsewhere Society.

Today, still tired from the night game, I participated in a panel discussion on the NPR show *On Point*. The subject was a *New York Times* article the previous Sunday that relayed the woes of high-earning women who find it difficult to date. In New York City (and presumably other urban areas), college-educated women in their twenties now outnumber college-educated men. What's more, for the first time, this group of women outearn their male counterparts. The result—claimed in the article, and by the other guests—was gender-role confusion. The women seemed frustrated that they couldn't find men who outearned them, or, alternatively, men who weren't intimidated by their high-powered jobs and designer labels. And, they added, it was never pleasant when the check arrived at the end of the dinner date.

My given role was to try to assuage their fears. The data just don't support their claims of frustration, I argued. Professional women are more likely to marry and stay married than are less-educated, lower-earning women. Their extended schooling careers, I tried to suggest, were the real culprits in their dating woes. They were, in effect, just *starting* the sorting/matching process that would predictably result in a match with a relatively high-earning spouse by the time they were in their late thirties (even if he didn't earn quite as much as they did). In fact, part of the inequality story is this increasing divergence between the marital patterns of high earners and low earners and the increasing precision with which educated men and women marry. The worries of Maureen Dowd—repeated often in her columns— are simply wrong, I tried to say; most professional men don't want to marry their secretaries—they want to marry a partner at the firm, too. True, the rates of college graduation for women have been going up as men's have been declining over the past three decades, so an increasing number of women will have to marry down and become the breadwinners of the household— but wasn't that part of the point of the feminist movement, after all? Dating norms and gender roles are highly plastic and will adapt to the new economic reality—if not for them, then for the group in college right now.

They wouldn't hear any of it. They knew what they knew from their own experiences and nobody could convince them otherwise.

As I hope is implied by these two anecdotes that took place within a single twenty-four-hour period, a slow and steady—yet fundamental—shift has occurred over the last thirty years in the way we work and live. The fans mugging for the camera and the plight of twenty-something executive women may appear, at first glance, to be totally unrelated realms of contemporary life. But, as I hope to have convinced you, they are in fact connected on a deeper level by the economic and social roots that have taken hold since the 1970s. These forces include the growth of women's work in the formal economy; the rise of information technology that allows many professionals to blend work and leisure on a 24/7 basis; and increasing inequality at the top of the ladder. No one of these trends is *the* root cause of the changes to the way we experience our daily lives today.

There is a paradox afoot in America. Partly thanks to technological changes, partly due to the spread of markets into every corner of our existence, and partly as a result of a grand historical trend, our society is becoming more efficient, rationalized, monetized, and priced for sale. This is in many ways a positive development. Greater efficiency means greater wealth for all.

After all, why did it take so long for Americans to decide that secondhand smoke is bad or that seat belts are good? They would seem like no-brainers, but it wasn't until the evidence mounted from careful, scientifically rationalized studies that pressure began to mount for such laws as mandatory seat belts. These studies take time. Greater efficiency means that more of this sort of knowledge can be generated faster (and faster), leading to better outcomes. And it is the hyperrational tool of cost-benefit analysis—the quintessential economic calculus—that allows for the articulation of the market with the public sphere. It wasn't until advocates could make a case that seat belts saved substantial "statistical" lives, and therefore money, that they could override the carmakers' insistence that they were an extra cost consumers weren't willing to bear. It wasn't until anti-smoking public health officials used the hidden language of contracts and externalities by focusing on the innocent third parties who suffer torts from the transactions between cigarette companies and smokers that they were successfully able to push for restrictions on where and when individuals could smoke.

But there is a hidden cost to all this efficiency and its corresponding economic logics that Max Weber first identified a century ago: Wealth accumulation and increased efficiency become ends in themselves. For example, instead of attaining success as a sign that we are saved—as our Puritan ancestors did—some of us now pray for salvation in order to strike it rich. Today, the highly educated, white-collar professional earns more per hour than ever before. However, instead of using that increased income to "live the good life," she now works more hours. Why? Because now that her billable rate is $200 per hour instead of $100, it "costs" her more to stay home and "do nothing." Never mind the loss of *social* capital that mothers (more than fathers) have typically provided their families through their unpaid work: better to stay at work for longer hours and buy child care services in the marketplace (where caring work is paid at a much lower rate in our increasingly unequal economy).

Alternatively, she can work from home, shifting attention back and forth between a game of catch and the writing of a memo to her sales staff. Add in a 24/7 information society where we can be online at any time—sprinkle some economic insecurity into the mix—and, voilà, literally each second not spent working in the marketplace is money lost. And of course, since she and her husband are working more at a higher rate of pay, inequality is increasing—further driving the race to the top.

Some things are priceless, argues the credit card ad; for everything else, there's MasterCard. Increasingly, you can charge even those so-called priceless experiences. Only in the most sacred aspects of life do we still resist the impulse to price the priceless (for now): organs (at least in the formal market), sex (ditto), and children. Elisabeth Lindes and Richard Posner famously argued that we'd be better off if we allowed a free market for children. Think about it: If someone is the top bidder on eBay for a child, aren't they likely to take better care of it, or at least provide it with the most materially comfortable lifestyle? And even more important, if someone is willing to offer their kid for sale, do we really want them to be a parent anyway?[1] Never mind typical concerns about the market being flooded (price corrections will take care of that). Just imagine the disciplining possibilities: "Son, if you don't do your homework, I'm going to put you on eBay!"

Likewise for our own flesh. Several years ago, I sat in on a health policy conference at which an economist got up to present a proposal for "treatment options" to allow for more freedom for patients. The particular issue the male economist addressed was breast cancer. As it turns out, he argued, the survival rate for a radical mastectomy was about the same as the survival rate for a lumpectomy. A mastectomy costs a lot less than a lumpectomy, however. So much less that the economist proposed giving patients the choice of opting for the mastectomy plus a check for several thousand dollars in lieu of the more costly lumpectomy. Nobody was being forced to do anything. Anyone could still choose the lumpectomy, just like before. But now they had a choice, thanks to a newly efficient market. Never mind that women of varying economic means faced starkly different calculations: If we don't like inequality, the solution is not to constrain choices, it's to have a more progressive tax policy. And never mind that many of the women in the audience mumbled that the economist should have studied testicular cancer.

All these phenomena are a result of commensurability: the fact that money is a universal medium that can price anything. It was wonderful in the time of Adam Smith. After all, with barter, how could you trade a cow for salt? You would be entitled to so much salt that you'd have to organize multiple trades to make the transaction happen. But with money, it's magic. Now every sale doesn't have to be a purchase at the same time. Money is freedom. Freedom to make our worldly goods disappear in a poof of green only to reappear later when we need them. But in today's totally connected economy, we can make anything disappear—even our breast. We can even trade things that are invisible themselves: How about some bond-backed bonds I have to offer you?

One problem with all of this efficient monetization is that the mere presence of pecuniary rewards tends to erode other motives for doing things. Psychologists have shown that when children are rewarded with prizes (money or treats) for academic performance and then those prizes are withdrawn, they lose their motivation to read, practice their instrument, do math, and so on.[2] Extrinsic motivation—money, in this case, but also fame, glory, what have you—tends to crowd out intrinsic motivation: doing something for the sheer pleasure of it or because you like to challenge yourself or some other reason that has little to do with other people. One can, then, only imagine how we might start viewing our own children and spouses if markets and economic incentives are allowed to penetrate any further into our homes. Although the markets for actual breast cancer treatment or for children may fail to take off, cancer and kid "futures" are more likely to emerge—that is, financial instruments that allow us to hedge risk on our own health and our children's future labor market earnings. Why not? Offspring outcomes are already important status markers for many families, so they are already goods, so to speak, in that high-stakes market we call the college admissions process.

There are other aspects of market rationalization that may have counterintuitive outcomes as well, and they have to do with time. One effect of the 24/7 economy is to erode what economists call *commitment devices*. The idea of a commitment device is intuitive to anyone who has ever dieted, tried to quit smoking, or finished an arduous homework assignment. You're going to put away that chocolate bar, which you really crave this very minute, until you are finished writing that long-overdue letter to grandma, as a way to induce yourself to finally "just do it." You join the expensive gym to add the monetary incentive to working out. You get on the Atkins diet and avoid carbohydrates altogether, since just trying to eat in moderation didn't really work out. Or you allow yourself to smoke only cigarettes that you "bum" off someone else; you are never allowed to actually buy a pack. In these instances, "you" play the role of the innocent bystander, collaterally damaged in the war between your multiple, intravidual selves.

Sometimes these tricks work, but other times one of your multiple selves convinces you that your barter doesn't really count as "buying," or that if you ask your friend to actually hand the money to the convenience store clerk for your smokes, then you are clear and free. You have to renegotiate the contract. Of course, some commitment mechanisms are more effective than others since we cannot get out of them. Jumping off a bridge is a better commitment to suicide than is taking pills, for instance. Buying a nonrefundable ticket is clearly a more effective mechanism than charging a refundable one.

Although we need these commitment mechanisms to self-manage—or rather, to manage our multiple selves—the irony lies in the fact that we need them now more than ever before, when we are bombarded with constant temptation ranging from junk food to personal services to cheap stuff on Skymall .com. And just as we need them more, they become less effective, thanks to market efficiency. Max out one credit card so you are forced to stop spending? A preapproved offer for a new one arrives in the mail that same day.

If you are looking for easy answers to this predicament, you've got the wrong book. I am not going to tell you to run out and buy an antique copy of the *Boy Scout Handbook* to recapture (and pass on) the simple pleasures of a bygone era such as orienteering with a compass, knotcraft, or star-gazing (the nighttime skies are probably too bright these days, anyway). I'm not going to suggest that you set an alarm so that you only allow yourself to check your e-mail twice a day. I am not even going to tell you—as my godfather recently instructed me—to leave your BlackBerry behind and go hike in Yosemite National Park (the national parks are probably too crowded, anyway). I am just going to cite the hackneyed idiom, "If you can't beat 'em, join 'em."

Do not hold yourself to a mythologized standard of the past in which everyone's attention was focused on only one task at a time. It turns out that when researchers studied engineers working in the early 1990s (before the BlackBerry era but after the advent of computers in their profession), the average time they spent focusing on a given task was about six seconds.[3] They didn't have e-mail to check, but they did have lots of other multitasking possibilities. Why only six seconds? Maybe this time limit is inherent to the nature of knowledge work. Thinking is, perhaps, like staring at a bright light. It's too intense, and you have to look away every so often. So go ahead; you have my permission to get up and make coffee, check your e-mail, or scratch yourself before you go on to the next sentence. I know I did.

I will thus indulge myself to make a single prediction in a book that has tried to avoid them throughout: Successful companies (and intraviduals) in the coming years will be the ones who—like Google—blend and bend rather than build walls between the domains of life. For example, rather than drop-off day care, a new model called "Two-rooms" offers office space for working parents separated only by glass from their toddlers, who explore a play space in the next room. The *kinder* are supervised by an adult, but the parents and children can wave, signal each other, and cross the divide as often as they want in between their respective block towers and e-mail messages. Likewise, we are already seeing that the successful political candidates tend to be the ones who integrate their family into their campaigns. The successful professional parents will be the ones who manage to blend their child-rearing duties with their professional ones, making their children comfortable in high-pressure, high-status work environments where big vocabulary words fly back and forth and the kids get used to the "family business," so to speak.[4]

However, while we shouldn't try to swim against the tides of history in our own lives, there do exist important, protective steps we should think about taking at the national level to protect the common interest. First of all, the rise of convestment— my term for the merger of consumption and investment—along with home offices and other economic phenomena that blur income-producing activity with income-reducing activity (i.e., spending) present an enormous challenge to the tax system. The IRS can tinker with the rules for deductions only so much; the deductors are always one step ahead. For example, new IRS rules are coming down the pike regarding the deductability of cell phones as a company expense. We may soon all need to carry around two: one for "clients" and the other to check on the kids. Of course, who's a "client" anyway? The IRS is fighting a pretty tough battle here.

Perhaps—dare I say it?—the time has come for simplifying the income tax and/or replacing all or part of it with a progressive value-added tax (VAT). Of course, a simplified income tax—even a flat tax—is likely to be gamed, too, since income is revenue minus expenses and expenses are where all the shenanigans go on. In fact, the VAT—common in Europe and elsewhere—itself is not immune to gaming. Even better than chasing and keeping track of flows of money might be to tax stagnant pools of it through the imposition of a national wealth tax, which could replace the current income tax system. In other words, each year, an individual is required to pay, say, 1 percent of their total net worth as of December 31. Though folks may complain that such a system might discourage investment and favor consumption, this issue could be addressed by combining a wealth tax with a sales tax or VAT on consumption.

The real issue is that though this is the most progressive form of taxation (since the distribution of wealth is even more uneven than the distribution of income), animosity toward wealth or property taxes dwarfs the resistance to all other forms of taxation (see, for example, Proposition 13 in California). Even the socialist-leaning Danes rebelled against property taxes—the only tax revolt in modern Europe! So, while there is no perfect solution, clearly something needs to be done when the late Leona Helmsley, worth hundreds of millions of dollars, could brag to her maid that "Only the little people pay taxes."[5] (Admittedly she went to jail for tax evasion on a conviction that some commentators claimed was a weak case motivated more by public scorn of her bad attitude.) That was almost twenty years ago. The loopholes have only grown bigger since.

The social provision side of things needs to be rethought as well. Social Security, for example, was originally intended as old-age insurance. That's right, insuring for the unfortunate possibility that you lived too long! Similarly, welfare was meant to keep widowed moms at home with their children. And besides, these New Deal programs were meant to provide basic necessities. They still do that, but Americans have come to expect more. For a long time, many large employers played that important role, providing generous, guaranteed health and retirement benefits. But that system, as we have seen, has collapsed under the weight of its own obligations. It is no more sensible today to expect private enterprise in a globally competitive economy to serve as our sugar daddy than it is to expect taxpayers to pay for poor women to stay home and take care of their kids when middle-class women are multitasking their brains out in the rat race. This is especially true when the very nature of work is changing. In shifting to profit sharing and defined contribution (401[k]) plans, industry is already ahead of government in this regard.

However, government has a role to play: to help Americans help themselves through policies that encourage savings and investment. For example, several proposals out there right now create universal savings accounts that enjoy tax-preferred status and receive matching funds from the government. Replacing the myriad plans currently available—Health Spending Accounts (HSAs); Roth IRAs, regular IRAs; 529 College Savings Plans; and so on—with one universal account that could be used for health, education, or retirement would go a long way in recognizing that in today's economy, elsewhere families need flexibility in how and when they need to draw down on their savings.

Aside from tax and social policy, we also need to rethink how we are going to protect the commons. This is an age-old problem from the days when there was literally a "commons"—unowned land that was shared by the community for grazing livestock. The basic paradox back in this pastoral yesteryear was pretty much the same as it is today: Everyone acting in their own interest leads to failure, or "the tragedy of the commons," since, without formal or informal restrictions, the land will become overgrazed to the point of desertification. The same is true for a wide range of common pool resources today: peace and quiet, a drive free from advertisements, clean air, spam-free Internet arteries, and even darkness so we can see the stars at night. One individual's freedom to "truck and barter" (as Adam Smith famously termed economic activity) increasingly impinges on many others' rights to be left alone (think junk mail). Likewise, an enormous amount of the costs of doing business are not born by the players involved but rather by the rest of us (think junk mail again, or plastic water bottles and landfill). What is different in the new economy is that as the market penetrates so many new facets of our lives and extends geographically around the globe, the scale and impact of these so-called externalities has grown since the commons is now so large.

An "externality" is simply defined as when someone who is not party to a contract is affected by its provisions—i.e., it's the result of an incomplete contract. The direct-mail marketer pays the postage to the government for the cost of delivering the catalogue to my mailbox but doesn't compensate me for the hassle of having to dispose of it, nor does it pay the cost to my municipality for the landfill space it takes up. Again, you may pay me a premium for my land since you plan to build a toxic chemical factory on it. But my neighbors didn't get a say in the transaction—or compensation for it—even though the chemical factory will affect their health and property values. Zoning is the standard solution to this particular problem. But in an increasingly interconnected and global economy, where externalities can span political jurisdictions and even entire continents, the potential externalities seem to multiply beyond control. When we ship bottled water over here from Fiji, there is not only the disposal of the plastic to worry about, there is also the damage to the Fiji fishing industry that must be considered, as well as the CO_2 and pollution that the entire process emits to the earth's atmosphere.

Some hard-core economists suggest a seemingly radical solution to this problem: Simply get rid of the commons by making everything into private property. If, for example, Rupert Murdoch owned the Pacific Ocean, then the Fiji water company would have to pay him for the right to use its shipping lanes, and the market would find the proper "cost" to that imposition. Environmentalists, in turn, could outbid the bottling company to prevent its use of the ocean. Similarly, if Murdoch or someone else owned the sky, then companies would pollute just the "right" amount since they would have to pay for that right at the going rate, and industries whose value produced didn't exceed that cost would die out. Obviously, we don't want Rupert Murdoch controlling our skies (any more than he already does). But what if the citizens of the United States (or the world) each owned one share of the sky? Based on the Alaska Permanent Fund, which distributes the revenue from that state's oil and other mineral resources, the "Skytrust" is one proposal that has been floated to concretize atmospheric property rights in order to enable collective decision making and profit sharing.

To sum up this policy discussion with a word for the wise: Folks who are concerned about the trampling of public space by private interests will not succeed in making nostalgic arguments about a bygone era of simpler lifestyles and wholesome values. What works is co-opting the language of markets and private contracts for the public good. Want to ban trans fats from your city's restaurants? Don't talk about how bad they are for the consumer. Talk about how much it costs the taxpayers for our *kids* to eat this stuff. And how much more it costs society when our children turn out more obese and dumber thanks to the effects of trans fats on young bodies and brains. Want to pass a stricter motorcycle helmet law? Don't use paternalistic language about saving reckless nuts from themselves. Talk about what a nuisance it is to everyone else to have to scrub brains off the freeway so often (and how much it ties up traffic). Want to ban cell phones from a public space? Make an argument about the loss in productivity associated with rude neighbors and the crime that results from distracted urban citizens. And if you want to resist the forced implementation of television screens in the backseat of taxicabs, then don't complain about their aesthetics or the invasion of once private space by commerce. Instead, whip up some talking points addressing the "principal-agent problem," in that the revenue stream does not go back to the cabdriver or the passenger but rather to a third party, who doesn't have to pay for their installation or suffer through their monotonous content. In short, if you can't beat the logic of the market, then join it—but on your own terms.

And keep in mind that every economy is built upon a paradox or two. In time, inevitably, these paradoxes become the death knell for a given system of production and distribution—though not usually unfolding in the way early naysayers had predicted it would.[6] For example, industrialization and its twin brother modern capitalism brought with them multiple contradictions. One was that it was in the capitalist's interest to drive down the wages of his workers in order to maximize profits. Sounds fine, except that since all capitalists are doing the same thing, there comes a situation in which hardly anyone can afford the products being produced. After all, the workers in the factories are also the economy's consumers. If they don't enjoy a "living wage," then they can't afford to keep the owners flush. Hence what Marx called "the crisis of overproduction" (something that Malthus would have found as believable as science fiction). These periodic crises would cause economic recessions or even depressions. They would be solved, in due time, through the conquest of new markets. For example, imperialism would sniff out Coke drinkers in far-off lands who could be tapped as consumers while providing more, better, and cheaper raw materials in return for their Big Macs. That would give a good jolt to the economy and get us back on the growth track. And if that didn't work, then a war or two would destroy enough capital and labor to right the system. Rinse and repeat as needed.

However, this wage earner/consumer tension was not the only paradox embedded in modern capitalism. Marx also pointed out the irony that a free market system of competition would eventually end in monopoly because "inferior" producers would be swallowed up by their competitors until the point at which only one capitalist or company reigned supreme (Microsoft, perhaps?). Of course, monopoly capitalism is just about the opposite of free market capitalism, and the entire logic of competition is thus undermined from within. Eventually, according to Marx, the crises of overproduction would become too severe as new markets dried up (i.e., as capitalism spread to the entire globe, leaving precious few new entrants to the system); likewise, the ownership structure would get so top-heavy as to keel over, leading to rule by the workers—a.k.a. communism.

Alas, history has not proceeded as Marx predicted.[7] But if

Marx is right insofar as the next ruling class is to be found lurking in the figurative back alleys of the old economy, we might ask: Who among us is the next ruling class? The Mexicans in the fields of Watsonville, California, picking our "organic" lettuce and asparagus? Probably not. We must keep in mind that the peasants—the serfs—did not rise to power with the downfall of feudalism. Rather, it was the merchant class. The next ruling class for our time is probably not at the bottom of our economic pyramid but rather off to the side somewhere. No-border activists? Perhaps we should ask who inhabits the abandoned spaces (social or physical) of the information economy once it starts to recede. Or, following the logic of the Coal Era and the Oil Century, we should look to energy for our clues. Increasingly, many individuals will be looking to move "off grid"— providing as much as possible of their own, self-sufficient power through wind, solar, and other means.

While I can't say specifically what the next decade will look like, I can share a general principle of how history moves forward that I borrow from the German philosopher Hegel: Each thesis generates its antithesis and then these merge to form a new thesis (the synthesis). In other words, we can already see the backlash to the Elsewhere Ethic emerging in the rise of green markets and the local foods movement, the slow food movement, the slow sex movement, and so on. This is to be expected, just as the 1950s gave rise to the seeds of the 1960s counterculture in the form of the beatniks. Eventually, the dominant and countercultures merged (synthesis) to give us the social ethic that reigns today. These alternative, slow-living movements will likely gain steam over the next few years but will ultimately merge into (and thereby alter) the mainstream Elsewhere Society. What that integration will look like I cannot predict.

Author's Note

It's the job of the sociologist to show us how, in the words of C. Wright Mills, our personal troubles are connected to public issues. Or, put another way by the sociologist Edward Shills, one of the jobs of sociology is to hold a mirror up to society. That has been the fundamental task of this book: to connect daily experience of the Elsewhere class to the larger historical changes that have occurred beneath our feet. Rather than holding up a mirror, or taking a snapshot of society, what I hope to do is more like taking an X-ray or an MRI, to reveal what is happening that is not normally visible. There are those who that will say that there is nothing new under the sun. In fact, that is also a principal job of the sociologist: to show how the more things change, the more they stay the same. And it is true that many of the elements of what I talked about in the preceding pages have been around for a long time—if not time immemorial. That said, it is also undeniable that a new social reality is upon us. In 1867, when Karl Marx wrote *Das Kapital,* there were no doubt critics who humbugged and claimed that there was nothing new about life in factory capitalism. But in retrospect we can see that industrial capitalism fundamentally altered human existence in a way that would have been unimaginable before.*

In that vein, while it is a relatively straightforward task for

---

*For this 1867 defense, I am indebted to Todd Gitlin.

me to marshal statistics to refute common claims we hear in the media—such as the notion that job security has declined for white-collar workers—it is not so easy to prove what I am claiming to be true in lieu of these common myths we tell ourselves. How can I definitively show that the rise in women's labor force participation is the driving force behind the blurring of work and home? Again, how can anyone be sure that it is rising inequality—combined with these eroding boundaries between realms of life—that generates intense anxiety among highly paid professionals, causing them to work harder than ever before? Or that these forces work in combination to create an epidemic of fraud anxiety among the upper classes? Or that the individualism of the modern era is giving way to an ethic of "intravidualism" in the networked economy? There is no statistical test or historical comparison that will establish these claims as social facts. This is not social science as I practice it in my day job, replete with falsifiable hypotheses, experimental methods, and the like. This is social criticism, and as such the real test lies with you, dear reader: Does what I argued in these pages strike you as spot on? Could I have been spying on your life or the lives of folks you know and interact with daily? Or, at the very least, does what I write seem plausible as you scan the wider social horizon around you? In short, do I make sense?

Acknowledgments

Many people, places, and things made this book possible. The first draft of a pre- preproposal was completed while lying on a mattress on a veranda in Nudgee Beach in Queensland, Australia, in the home of my brother- and sister-in-law, Andrew Jeremijenko and Michele Dahl. So I must thank them for their generous hospitality that allowed this project to germinate. Enormous thanks also go to my agent, Sydelle Kramer, of the Susan Rabiner agency, who went back and forth with me many times turning a mess of incoherent ideas into an actual book proposal. Dan Frank, my longtime editor at Pantheon, deserves my enormous gratitude for further encouraging and shaping the ultimate product. His support was enormous, going so far as to abrogate a former book contract for a never-realized and long-overdue book on the relationship between physical appearance and socioeconomic status. He wiped the proverbial slate clean and welcomed this new *Elsewhere* child into his midst with open arms.

Other folks who read the book and provided helpful comments along the way include (in alphabetical order), Mitchell Duneier, Doug Guthrie, Natalie Jeremijenko (who is also a character in the book), Gerald Marwell, Harvey Molotch, and Richard Sennett. Todd Gitlin was also helpful, through lunchtime discussions, in framing many of these issues. Of course, the copy editor, Ann Adelman, did a great job of fixing not just my grammar but also my logic in certain instances. And as the devil is in the details of any researched book, big, big thanks go out to Lauren Marten, who proofed several drafts and highlighted every claim, fact, or opinion in the book, forcing me to either back it up with the proper citation or delete it from the manuscript. What's more, she was often the one who had to find the relevant quotation, statistic, or reference from some obscure government report or journal article, of which I only had the fuzziest recollection as guidance of where to look.

With this Herculean search effort in mind, I want to thank Google twice: firstly for hosting me at the 2007 SciFoo camp, where I got to experience their corporate culture up close; and secondly, for making Lauren's and my job easier when it came time to dig up long-forgotten citations. Thanks also go out to JSTOR on this front. And as long as I am thanking institutions, I have to express my appreciation to New York University for providing a fertile environment for this kind of more public work and for valuing it, perhaps in a way that other universities might not. In this vein, particular thanks go out to Richard Foley, the dean of the Faculty of Arts and Sciences; to George Downs, the dean of Social Science; to David McLaughlin, NYU's provost; and to NYU President John Sexton. For administrative support with this project I also have to thank Alana Barraj and Dom Bagnato here at NYU, and at Pantheon Books, Dan Frank's assistant, Fran Bigman. And for always asking why and keeping me guessing, I have to thank my kids, E and Yo Jeremijenko-Conley.

Notes

INTRODUCTION

1. Suzanne M. Bianchi, John P. Robinson, and Melissa A. Milkie, *Changing Rhythms of American Family Life* (New York: Russell Sage Foundation, 2007). See also, Anne H. Gauthier, Timothy M. Smeeding, and Frank F. Furstenberg, Jr., "Are Parents Investing Less Time in Children? Trends in Selected Industrialized Countries," *Population and Development Review* 30, no. 4 (December 2004): 647–71.

2. Edward Woff, Wealth Inequality Calculations, 2009. New York University, Department of Economics.

3. David Brauer, "What Accounts for the Decline in Manufacturing Employment?" figure 3. U.S. Congressional Budget Office, February 2004. See also, U.S. Department of State's Bureau of International Information Programs, "A Service Economy," U.S.A. Economy in Brief at http://usinfo.state.gov/products/pubs/economy-in-brief/page3.html.

4. "Income Inequality Measures," in *Luxembourg Income Study*, May 27, 2003, at http://www.lisproject.org/keyfigures/ineqtable.htm.

5. Paul Krugman, "For Richer," *New York Times Magazine*, October 20, 2002.

6. Jacob Hacker, *The Great Risk Shift* (New York and London: Oxford University Press, 2006).

7. Steven G. Allen, Robert L. Clark, and Sylvester A. Schieber, "Has Job Security Vanished in Large Corporations?," in *On The Job: Is Long-Term Employment a Thing of the Past?*, ed. David Neumark (New York: Russell Sage Foundation, 2000).

8. Calculated from "Fertility and Family Surveys," 1995 National Survey of Family Growth.

9. Suzanne Bianchi and Sara Raley, "Time Allocation in Families," in *Work, Family, Health, and Well-Being*, ed. Suzanne M. Bianchi, Lynne M. Casper, and Rosalind Berkowitz King (New York: Routledge, 2005), p. 35.

10. Daniel S. Hammermesh and Jungmin Lee, "Stressed Out on Four Continents: Time Crunch or Yuppie Kvetch?," NBER Working Paper no. 10186, National Bureau of Economic Research, Cambridge, Mass., December 2003.

11. Claude Fisher, "Ever-More Rooted Americans," *City & Community* 1 (June 2002): 174–94.

12. U.S. Census Bureau, Housing and Household Economic Statistics Division, "Historical Census of Housing Tables," 2004, at http://www.census.gov/hhes/www/housing/census/historic/owner.html.

13. Housing Vacancies and Homeownership: Table 5, Homeownership Rates for the United States: 1968 to 2009," *US Census Bureau, Housing and Household Economic Statistics Division.*

14. James Traub, "The Measures of Wealth," *New York Times Magazine,* October 14, 2007, p. 22.

15. Peter Kuhm and Fernando Lozano, "The Expanding Workweek? Understanding Trends in Long Work Hours Among U.S. Men, 1979–2004," *Journal of Labor Economics* (December 2005).

16. Mike Males, "This Is Your Brain on Drugs, Dad." *New York Times* op-ed, January 3, 2007.

FROM THE PROTESTANT ETHIC TO THE ELSEWHERE ETHIC

1 Manfred F. R. Kett de Vries, "The Dangers of Feeling Like a Fake," *Harvard Business Review* (September 2005): 108–16.

2 See Sharon R. Cohany and Emy Sok, "Trends in Labor Force Participation of Married Mothers of Infants," *Monthly Labor Review Online* 130, no. 2 (2007).

3. Jeffrey J. Sallaz, *The Labor of Luck: Work and Politics in the Global Gambling Industry* (Berkeley: University of California Press, forthcoming 2009).

4. Natasha Schüll, *Machine Life: Control and Compulsion in Las Vegas* (Princeton, N.J.: Princeton University Press, forthcoming 2009).

5. Geoffrey Gray, "With This Ring (and This Contract), I Thee Wed," *New York,* March 19, 2006.

AND YOU MAY FIND YOURSELF BEHIND THE WHEEL
OF A LARGE AUTOMOBILE

1. "Oil Crises and Climate Challenges: 30 Years of Energy Use in IEA Countries," International Energy Agency, p. 37, fig. 3.1, 2004.

2. Herbert J. Gans, *The Levittowners: Ways of Life and Politics in a New Suburban Community* (New York: Pantheon Books, 1967).

3. Department of Defense, "Charles E. Wilson," Secretary of Defense Histories, at http://www.defenselink.mil/specials/secdef_histories/bios/wilson.htm.

4. David Halberstam, *The Fifties* (New York: Ballantine, 1993). See pp. 117–20 for a wonderful, more thorough discussion of the Oil Century and GM; this quote from the top of p. 119.

5. Gerald Mayer, *Union Membership Trends in the United States*, Congressional Research Service Report, Library of Congress, 2004.

6. See, e.g., my first book, *Being Black, Living in the Red: Race, Wealth and Social Policy in America* (Berkeley: University of California Press, 1999).

7. Shawna Orzechowski and Peter Sepielli, "Net Worth and Asset Ownership of Households: 1998 and 2000," *Household Economic Studies*, U.S. Census Bureau, May 2003.

8. Author's calculations from Bureau of Labor Statistics data. See "Construction NAICS 23," Industries at a Glance Workforce Statistics at http://www.bls.gov/iag/tgs/iag23.htm#workforce.

9. American Council for an Energy-Efficient Economy, *Blackouts and the Big Picture*, 2003, at http://www.aceee.org/press/0309mgkblkout.htm.

10. Avery M. Guest, "Patterns of Suburban Population Growth, 1970–75," *Demography* 16, no. 3 (1979).

11. Malcolm Jones, Jr., "Air Conditioning," *Newsweek*, December 2, 1997.

12. Ibid.

13. Nick Paumgarten, "Annals of Transportation: There and Back Again: The Soul of the Commuter," *The New Yorker*, April 16, 2007.

14. Clara Reschovsky, "Journey to Work: 2000," *Census 2000 Brief*, 2004, and "Travel Time to Work for the United States: 1990 and 1980 Census," Population Division, U.S. Census Bureau, at http://www.census.gov/population/socdemo/journey/ustime.txt.

15. "Historical Census of Housing," U.S. Census Bureau, *Census of Housing, 2004*, at http://www.census.gov/hhes/www/housing/census/historic/owner.html.

16. Dalton Conley and Brian Gifford, "Home Ownership, Social Insurance and the Welfare State," *Sociological Forum* 21, no. 1 (March 2006): 55–82.

17. "Highlights of Annual 2006 Characteristics of New Housing: Manufacturing, Mining and Construction Statistics," U.S. Census Bureau, at http://www.census.gov/const/www/highanncharac2006.html.

18. Pamela J. Perun, "Towards a Sensible System for Saving," for the Aspen Institute-Initiative on Financial Security, Washington, D.C., 2006.

19. Michael Carliner, "Housing and GDP," National Association of Home Builders, 2001.

20. Carter B. Horsley, "Loft Conversions Exceeding New Apartment Construction," *New York Times,* October 12, 1980.

21. Richard Florida, *The Rise of the Creative Class and How It's Transforming Work, Leisure, Community and Everyday Life* (New York: Basic Books, 2002).

22. Deborah Blumenthal, "At Work They Are at Home," *New York Times,* July 15, 1979.

23. Richard D. Lyons, "If You're Thinking of Living in: Murray Hill," *New York Times,* April 12, 1987.

24. Deborah Blumenthal, "At Work They Are at Home," *New York Times,* July 15, 1979.

25. "Personal Finance: Using Home as Office Space," *New York Times,* March 20, 1979.

26. Consuelo Laude Kertz and Al L. Hartgraves, "The Home-Office Deduction," *Academe* 73, no. 1 (January-February 1987): 20–24.

27. *Commissioner of Internal Revenue, Petitioner v. Nader E. Soliman,* January 12, 1993. Available at Cornell University Law School Supreme Court Collection, http://www.law.cornell.edu/supct/html/91-998.ZO.html.

28. "A History of American Agriculture." 2007, at http://inventors .about.com/library/inventors/blfarm4.htm; and U.S. Environmental Protection Agency, "Demographics," 2006, at http://www.epa.gov/oecaagct/ag101/ demographics.html.

29. "Home Office: Tax Perk or Trap? A third of U.S. employees regularly work out of a home office but most don't claim a deduction," CNN, February 17, 2005.

30. Steven Weyhrich, "Apple II History," November 12, 2001, at http://apple2history.org/history/ah01.html; "Commodore PET," at http:// oldcomputers.net/pet2001.html; Jeremy Reimer, "Total Share: 30 Years of Personal Computer Market Share Figures," *Arts Technica,* December 14, 2005, at http://arstechnica.com/articles/culture/total-share.ars/4.

31. Valerie A. Ramey and Francis Neville, "A Century of Work and Leisure," NBER Working Paper no. 12264, 2006.

32. Peter Kuhn and Fernando Lozano, "The Expanding Workweek? Understanding Trends in Long Work Hours Among U.S. Men, 1979–2004," *Journal of Labor Economics* (December 2005): 311–43.

33. Daniel S. Hammermesh and Jungmin Lee, "Stressed Out on Four Continents: Time Crunch or Yuppie Kvetch?," NBER Working Paper no. 10186, 2003.

34. Ann Huff Stevens, "The More Things Change, the More They Stay the Same: Trends in Long-Term Employment in the United States," NBER Working Paper no. 11878, 2005.

35. Arlie Russell Hochschild, *The Time Bind: When Work Becomes Home and Home Becomes Work* (New York: Metropolitan Books, 1997).

36. Markus Mobius and Raphael Schoenle, "The Evolution of Work," NBER Working Paper no. 12694, 2006.

37. Frank Levy and Richard J. Murnane, *The New Division of Labor: How Computers Are Creating the Next Job Market* (Princeton, N.J.: Princeton University Press, 2004.).

38. Ibid., p. 38.

39. "Employment Status of Women and Men in 2006," Women's Bureau, U.S. Department of Labor, at http://www.dol.gov/wb/factsheets/Qf-ESWM06.htm.

40. Alison Owings, *Hey, Waitress!: The USA From the Other Side of the Tray* (Berkeley: University of California Press, 2002.).

41. Christine Schwartz, "Earnings Inequality and the Changing Association Between Spouses' Earnings," Working Paper no. 2007-13, Center for Demography and Ecology, University of Wisconsin at Madison, 2007.

42. Internal Revenue Service, "Table A —U.S. individual income tax: personal exemptions and lowest and highest bracket tax rates, and tax base for regular tax, tax years 1913–2003" (Rev. 4-2003), in *Statistics of Income Bulletin*, Publication 1136 (Winter 2002–03).

43. In 1948, 35 percent of women ages 25 to 54 worked outside the home. By 1955 this had risen to 39.8 percent and by 1960 stood at 42.9 percent and continued to rise from there. See Abraham Mosisa and Steven Hipple, "Trends in Labor Force Participation in the United States," *Monthly Labor Review* (October 2006): table 1, 36.

44. "Who We Are: A Profile of the UAW Membership by Sector," at http://www.uaw.org/about/members.html.

45. See Ivan Szelenyi and George Konrad, *Intellectuals on the Road to Class Power*, for a great discussion of the Hungarian case.

ONE PLUS A HUNDRED ZEROS

1. Posted by sutekichi on http://www.youtube.com/watch?v=KZASRm fUMOk; accessed August 9, 2007.

2. Posted by SimUK on http://www.youtube.com/watch?v=KZASRm fUMOk; accessed August 9, 2003.

3. Rachel Sherman. *Class Acts: Service and Inequality in Luxury Hotels* (Berkeley: University of California Press, 2007).

CONVESTMENT

1. Ronald Inglehart, *The Silent Revolution: Changing Values and Political Styles Among Western Publics* (Princeton, N.J.: Princeton University Press, 1977). See also Ronald Inglehart, "The Silent Revolution in Post-Industrial Societies," *American Political Science Review* 65 (1971): 991–1017. Ted Nordhaus and Michael Shellenberger elaborate on Inglehart's concept in their book *Break Through* to suggest that we now live in a condition of "insecure affluence." See, Ted Nordhaus and Michael Shellenberger, *Break Through: From the Death of Environmentalism to the Politics of Possibility* (New York: Houghton Mifflin, 2007).

2. Fred Hirsch, *The Social Limits to Growth* (London: Routledge & Kegan Paul, 1976).

3. Hirsch paraphrased in Robert L. Heilbroner, "The False Promise of Growth," *New York Review of Books* 24 (1977):10–12.

4. Chris Anderson, *The Long Tail: Why the Future of Business Is Selling Less of More* (New York: Hyperion, 2006).

5. Tibor Scitovsky, *The Joyless Economy: The Psychology of Human Satisfaction and Consumer Dissatisfaction* (New York: Oxford University Press, 1976).

6. Peter Kuhm and Fernando Lozano, "The Expanding Workweek? Understanding Trends in Long Work Hours Among U.S. Men, 1979–2004." *Journal of Labor Economics* (December 2005): 311–43.

7. Hannah Fairfield, "Pushing Paper Out the Door," *The New York Times*, February 10th, 2008, at http://www.nytimes.com/2008/02/10/business/10 metrics.html?pagewanted=1&_r=1.

8. Ronna Larsen, "The Skyrocketing Number of Bank Branches," *e-merging Directions*, Colliers Turley Martin Tucker Commerical Real Estate Services, at http://www.ctmt.com/pdfs/emergingDirections/BankBranches Skyrocket.pdf.

9. Juliet Schor, "The Social Death of Things," working paper, 2007.

10. Barry Schwartz, *The Paradox of Choice: Why More Is Less* (New York: HarperCollins, 2004).

SHOOT THE MOON

1. Jane Jacobs, *The Death and Life of Great American Cities* (New York: Vintage Books, 1961).

2. For this observation I must credit Natalie Jeremijenko's research in "Share This Book" (PhD diss., University of Queensland, Aust.).

3. "A Guide to UHF Television Production," 2004–2007, at http://www.indiana.edu/~radiotv/wtiu/uhf.shtml.

4. Ian Grey, "Tee-Construction: A Brief History of the T-Shirt," at http://www.vintageskivvies.com/pages/archives/articles/readersubmissions/history ofthet-shirt.html.

5. I need to cite the stepfather of my colleague Harvey Molotch for this insight.

6. Jocelyne Daw, *Cause Marketing for Nonprofits: Partner for Purpose, Passion, and Profits* (Hoboken, N.J.: John Wiley, 2006), chapter 1, at http://media.wiley.com/product_data/excerpt/09/04717175/0471717509.pdf.

7. http://www.gapinc.com/red/why_red.html; accessed August 29, 2007.

8. http://www.stopchildpoverty.org/learn/bigpicture/health/.

9. Leah Hoffman, "Most Charitable States," Forbes.com, November 2005.

10. Kennard T. Wing, Thomas H. Pollak, Amy Blackwood, *The Nonprofit Almanac 2008*, Urban Institute Press, Washington, D.C. 2008.

11. See, e.g., Johns Hopkins Comparative Nonprofit Sector Project, "Private Philanthropy Across the World," at http://www.jhu.edu/cnp/pdf/comptable5_dec05.pdf.

FROM ELSEWHERE TO NOWHERE

1. Federal Bureau of Invesitgation Uniform Crime Reporting, "Supplementary Homicide Reports, 1976–2005."

2. "Rambler History, 1902–1969," at http://amcrc.com/history/history.htm.

3. Liz Gaff, "NYPD Has iPod Etching Program," August 9, 2006, at http://www.gazette.com/rews/2006/0809/features/013.html; see also, www.nyc.gov/html/nypd/html/housing_bureau/psa2.shtml.

4. FBI Uniform Crime Reports, "United States Crime Rates, 1960–2006."

5. Jeff Manza and Christopher Uggen, *Locked Out: Felon Disenfranchisement and American Democracy* (New York: Oxford University Press, 2006).

6. Franklin E. Zimring, *The Great American Crime Decline* (New York: Oxford University Press, 2007).

7. S. Morgan Friedman, "The Inflation Calculator," at http://www.westegg.com/inflation/infl.cgi.

8. "Changing Perceptions of Body Weight Feed Rise in Obesity," August 6, 2007, at http://www.huliq.com/29508/changing-perceptions-of-body-weight-feed-rise-in-obesity.

9. Isabel V. Sawhill and Daniel P. McMurrer, "Declining Economic Opportunity in America," *The Future of the Public Sector,* The Urban Institute, Washington, D.C. (April 1996).

10. Jerry Hausman, "Cellular Telephone, New Products and the CPI," *Journal of Business and Economic Statistics* 17, no. 2 (1999): 188–94.

11. Laurence H. Holland and David Ewalt, "How Americans Make and Spend Their Money," at http://www.forbes.com/commerce/2006/07/19/spending-income-level_cx_lh_de_0719spending.html.

12. Ibid.

13. Amanda Lenhart, "Cyberbullying and Online Teens," Pew Internet and American Life Project, at http://www.pewinternet.org/PPF/r/216/report_display.asp, accessed June 27, 2007.

14. http://www.internetfraud.usdoj.gov/; accessed July 5, 2007.

POLYMORPHOUS PERVERSITY

1. A. E. Parkins, "The Temperature Region Map," *Annals of the Association of American Geographers* 16, no. 3 (September 1926): 151–65.

2. "Income Inequality Measures," *Luxembourg Income Study,* May 27, 2003, at http://www.lisproject.org/keyfigures/ineqtable.htm.

3. William Julius Wilson, *The Truly Disadvantaged: The Inner City, the Underclass and Public Policy* (Chicago: University of Chicago Press, 1987).

4. Lawrence L. Wu and Barbara Wolfe, ed., *Out of Wedlock: Cause and Consequences of Nonmarital Fertility* (New York: Russell Sage Foundation, 2001). See also, Trudi J. Renwick, *Poverty and Single Parent Families: A Study of Minimal Subsistence Household Budgets* (New York: Routledge, 1998).

5. Pamela J. Smock, "Remarriage Patterns of Black and White Women: Reassessing the Role of Educational Attainment," *Demography* 27, no. 3 (August 1990): 467–73.

6. Michael C. Keeley, "The Effects of Experimental Negative Income Tax Programs on Marital Dissolution: Evidence from the Seattle and Denver Income Maintenance Experiments," *International Economic Review* 28, no. 1 (February 1987).

7. Susan Thistle, *From Marriage to the Market: The Transformation of Women's Lives and Work* (Berkeley: University of California Press, 2006).

8. The National Center for Health Statistics, at http://nchspressroom.wordpress.com/tag/mothers/; see also David E. Williams, "More Hurdles as Women

Delay Birth, CNN.com, April 24, 2006, at http://www.cnn.com/2006/US/04/21/later.childbirth/.

9. Priscilla R. Carver and Iheoma U. Iruka, "After School Programs and Activities: 2005," in *National Household Education Surveys Program of 2005*, National Center for Education Statistics, Washington, D.C., May 2006.

10. For more on this debate, see Sara Bennett and Nancy Kalish, *The Case Against Homework: How Homework Is Hurting Our Children and What We Can Do About It* (New York: Crown, 2006); Alfie Kohn, *The Homework Myth* (New York: De Capo Press, 2006); and Harris M. Cooper, *The Battle Over Homework: Common Ground for Administrators, Teachers, and Parents* (Thousand Oaks, Calif.: Corwin Press, 2007).

11. Navarro, Mireya, "Pay Up, Kid, Or Your Igloo Melts," *New York Times*, October 28, 2007.

12. Annette Lareau, *Unequal Childhood: Class, Race and Family Life* (Berkeley: University of California Press, 2003).

13. Jason DeParle, *American Dream: Three Women, Ten Kids, and a Nation's Drive to End Welfare* (New York: Viking, 2004).

14. Amy Hsin, "Mothers' Time with Children and the Social Reproduction of Cognitive Skills" (unpublished paper, Dept. of Sociology, Univ. of California, Los Angeles, n.d.).

15. This literature is voluminous but see, for example, the famous Perry Preschool study that followed a treatment and control group of toddlers up through age forty in L. J. Schweinhart, J. Montie, Z. Xiang, W. S. Barnett, C. R. Belfield, and M. Nores, *Lifetime Effects: The High/Scope Perry Preschool Study Through Age 40* (Ypsilanti, Mich.: High/Scope Press, 2005).

16. David S. Bickham, Elizabeth A. Vandewater, Aletha C. Huston, June H. Lee, Allison Gilman Caplovitz, and John C. Wrigh, "Predictors of Children's Electronic Media Use: An Examination of Three Ethnic Groups," *Media Psychology* (2003): 107–37.

17. Mitchell Stevens, *Creating a Class: College Admissions and the Education of Elites* (Cambridge: Harvard University Press, 2007).

18. The Waldorf education system, conceived by Rudolf Steiner, was designed for the children of employees at the Waldorf Astoria cigarette factory in Germany at the request of the factory's owner.

THE BIRTH OF THE INTRAVIDUAL

1. We can see this devolution of the self into conflicting parts in the way we talk about theories of the self—both mind and body. In neuroscience, for

instance, examination of neurons and particular areas of the brain has largely been trumped by the now hotter approach of looking at neural networks in which memories, thoughts, and mental processes don't happen in specific places (i.e., neurons or sulcuses) but rather exist in the network of connections. The network is not reducible to the sum of its parts. Evidently, that goes for our own minds.

This decentering of the self can be seen in other experiments as well. Scientists made big news when they used virtual reality glasses and carefully positioned cameras to induce the same out-of-body experiences that near-death survivors have long reported in legend, for example, see B. Lenggenhager, T. Tadi, T. Metzinger, and O. Blanke "Video Ergo Sum: Manipulating Bodily Self-Consciousness," *Science* 317, no. 5841 (2007): 1096–99. The studies are built on what's called the "rubber hand" illusion. In this setup, an individual places one hand on her lap out of sight. A rubber hand is then placed on the table and both the "real" and fake hands are simultaneously stroked. The parallax between the seen and felt creates the illusion that the hand on the table is the real one (and the invisible one is forgotten about). This can be so effective that when researchers then smash the rubber hand with a hammer, subjects often cry out in pain, discussed in Matthew Botvinick and Jonathan Cohen, "Rubber Hands 'Feel' Touch That Eyes Can See," *Nature* 351, no. 756 (February 1998). Two research teams took the illusion a few steps further by using projected images of the entire body, combined with touching, to evince a similar dissociation of the self from the entire physical body. According to one scientist who commented on the studies, "the research reveals that 'the sense of having a body, of being in a bodily self,' is actually constructed from multiple sensory streams." See, Sandra Blakeslee, "Studies Report Inducing Out-of-Body Experience," *New York Times*, August 24, 2007. It's not that this experiment would have yielded different results in prior epochs, merely that its technology—and more important the impulse to perform it—is a product of our time.

Perhaps it is no coincidence that the major developmental syndrome of our time is autism—a disease or condition that is defined by the lack of (social) self. By age four or so, most kids pass the "cookie test": An experimenter puts two cookies in a box. Another, confederate experimenter who was present then leaves the room. While she is gone, the first experimenter allows the child to eat one of the cookies (or just gets rid of it somehow). When the confederate returns, the experimenter asks the child how many cookies the person who was out of the room thinks are in the box. Most children answer "two," since they are able to place themselves in the shoes of the other person and realize that the confederate should really have no idea that one of them is now gone since she didn't see it happen herself and otherwise has no way of knowing (no crumbs are left around). It is the ability to take the role of the other—as we have seen—that allows the self to develop since the self boils down to ability to perceive the "me" as distinct from the "I." That is, before you can see yourself as a self—as how others might view you—the first step is to learn that they do indeed have their own points of view. This is something that the social philosopher George Herbert Mead pointed out almost a hundred years ago. It is also something readily apparent to anyone who has watched a toddler (who has not yet fully developed a sense of the other and the self) play peek-a-boo. When he or she covers their eyes, they think that you can't see them.

Autistics, however, are stuck in this pre-social selfhood and cannot take the point of view of others so easily; in fact, when someone attempts to point out something to them, they often stare at the fingertip rather than the object at which it is aimed. These kids answer that the other person thinks that there is only one cookie in the box since there is only one cookie in the box. No amount of reasoning or explaining that the other person could not have known about the cookie being gone works. In order to grasp that, one must have a "concept of mind"—to use the phraseology of the psychologists. It is thus the act of empathizing with others that creates our own self.

Perhaps it should not be surprising that in an era where social networking is everything, those kids who can't socialize so easily, who can't take the role of the other, are diagnosed as lacking or deviant or maladapted in some way. In a less connected society, their "defects" might not matter so much. But in our time, the lack of social ability appears dire indeed. Or maybe the story is reversed: Is it the one-way mirror aspect of the looking-glass self that has caused (in part) the autism epidemic? In trying to explain the dramatic rise in autistic spectrum disorders researchers have blamed vaccines, environmental toxins, television viewing, and even reclassification of other disorders (mainly mental retardation) into the newly expansive autism category. They have not, perhaps, considered the more fundamental changes in social relations that we are *all* going through.

2. Theda Skocpol, "Civic Transformation and Inequality in the Contemporary United States," in *Social Inequality*, ed. Kathryn M. Neckerman (New York: Russell Sage Foundation, 2004), pp. 729–68.

3. Stanley Milgram, "The Small World Problem," *Psychology Today*, May 1967, pp. 60–67.

4. Mark S. Granovetter, "The Strength of Weak Ties," *American Journal of Sociology* 78, no. 6 (May 1973): 1360–80.

5. Damon Centola, Robb Willer, and Michael Macy, "The Emperor's

Dilemma: A Computational Model of Self-Enforcing Norms," *American Journal of Sociology* 110, no. 4 (January 2005): 1009–40.

CONCLUSION

1. Elisabeth M. Landes and Richard A. Posner, "The Economics of the Baby Shortage," *Journal of Legal Studies* 7, no. 2 (1978): 323–48.

2. Barry Schwartz., *The Paradox of Choice: Why More Is Less* (New York: HarperCollins, 2004).

3. Vinod Baya, "Information-Handling Behavior of Designers During Conceptual Design" (thesis, Stanford University, 1996).

4. Here I must confess to years of screaming at my wife for trying to involve the kids in her work life as well as yelling at her to turn off her cell phone during "family time." I was wrong, and she was right (on average, for professional parents, perhaps, with a host of other caveats as well). But I can't bring myself to apologize in the main text, so I am relegating this to an endnote.

5. Jun Fletcher, "For Mansion Owners, A Little-Noticed Tax Break," *The Wall Street Journal*, December 5, 1997.

6. The fundamental paradox in agrarian societies was identified by Thomas Malthus: Food production increased arithmetically (gradually) but human populations increase geometrically (i.e., like rabbits multiplicatively). This fact, according to Malthus, would yield a situation of near-constant human misery. Any improvement in agricultural technology would lead humans to have more babies and thus erase any improvement in living standards. We were doomed to cycles of mass starvation, war, and pestilence—all of which were necessary to cull the population. (In fact, living standards were never better than right after a big plague or war.) While Malthus could be said to have been right for most of the 13,000 years of human history during which the domestication of plants and animals has taken place, he certainly did not anticipate two phenomena: (1) the Agricultural (and Industrial) revolutions, which greatly improved living standards through increased production; and (2) the demographic transition, which slowed the rate of human population growth. The interplay of these two developments in human history is complicated and the source of much debate; needless to say, humans are not the mindless copulating rabbits that Malthus had presupposed. In fact, the average number of children started declining in the West well before modern contraception was available. We have seen demographic transitions—coupled with economic development—in other areas of the globe such as Asia and Latin America of late.

Meanwhile, in the effort to produce more food on limited land, technologies like crop rotation and the seed drill soon led to industrial technologies, which, in turn, led to urbanization (the agglomeration of human populations in cities to work in factories) and the gradual end of the agrarian lifestyle.

7. Marx, for example, didn't anticipate the rise of antitrust regulation that would break up the inevitable monopolies that formed from time to time. And he didn't foresee the important role that trade unions and labor laws would play in maintaining minimal wage levels and caps on worker hours. Nor could he have known about employee stock and pension plans that effectively gave workers a stake—albeit a much slimmer slice than major shareholders—in the profits of their company.

Index

advertising, advertisements, 94, 173
  cause marketing and, 121–3
  Elsewhere Ethic and, 25, 28, 32
  Google and, 102–4
  and marketing to captive audiences, 106–7, 110–13, 125
  public space and, 110–14, 118, 186, 188
  on T-shirts, 116–19
Africa, 82, 97*n*, 122, 141–3, 148
air-conditioning (AC), 45–7, 63
alienation, 16, 39, 100
  ethics and, 21–2, 24, 26–9, 33, 36
Allen, Woody, 164
Amazon, 162–5, 167
American Airlines (AA), 25
American Express (Amex), 25, 112, 121–2
Anderson, Chris, 93–4, 119, 163
Annie Hall, 164
apparel, 96–7, 116–18
artists, xi, 48–50, 65–6
Audible.com, 24
authority, 75–80
  charismatic, 75–8
  children and, 77, 79, 84, 152
  legal-rational, 75–7, 79–80
autism, 159, 204*n*–5*n*

behavioral change, 170–1
BlackBerrys, 51, 136, 167, 182
  Elsewhere class and, 4–5, 7, 10
  Elsewhere Ethic and, 23, 29, 32
blacks, 112, 118, 158–9, 161
  family life and, 145–6
  intravidualism and, 44, 63
Bloomberg, Michael, 66, 73–4
Blumenthal, Deborah, 50
book recommendations, 162–5, 167
bottled water, 123, 173, 186–7
Brin, Sergey, 66, 72, 77
Bureau of Labor Statistics, 134–5

capitalism, capitalists, 6, 10, 19–20 32, 34, 36, 85, 111, 189–91
  authority and, 75–6
  ethics and, 19–20
  intravidualism and, 42, 57, 65
  Marx on, 27, 38, 40, 190–1
cars, 33, 46–7, 118, 154, 165, 177–8
  crime and, 126–7, 132–3, 137, 139–40
  Elsewhere class and, 3–5, 15
  intravidualism and, 39–41, 43–4, 47, 59, 64–5
  positional goods and, 100–1
  public space and, 108–9

ALSO BY DALTON CONLEY

HONKY

Little league baseball, playground "snaps," and after school karate lessons—at first glance Dalton Conley's childhood had all the typical hallmarks of growing up. But on closer look, Conley's childhood was anything but normal. One of the few white boys in a neighborhood of mostly black and Puerto Rican housing projects on Manhattan's Lower East Side, Conley learned early on about race in America. His first lesson came at age three when he attempted to kidnap his neighbor—a black infant he was convinced could be his biological sister. By the time he was a teenager, he learned that even a doting parent couldn't keep his best friend from being stuck by a stray bullet. Since Conley's parents retained the "cultural capital" of the white middle class, Conley was able to move beyond the expectations of those in his community. Now a sociologist, Conley looks back on his childhood with remarkable insight. The result is a perfectly pitched memoir rich with moving portraits of people caught up in the vortex of race and class in America.

Memoir/978-0-375-72775-7

THE PECKING ORDER
*A Bold New Look at How Family and Society
Determine Who We Become*

In this groundbreaking and meticulously researched book, Dalton Conley shatters our notions of how our childhoods affect us, and why we become who we are. Economic and social inequality among adult siblings is not the exception, Conley asserts, but the norm: over half of all inequality is *within* families, not *between* them. And it is each family's own "pecking order" that helps to foster such disparities. Moving beyond traditionally accepted theories such as birth order or genetics to explain family dynamics, Conley instead draws upon three major studies to explore the impact of larger social forces that shape each family and the individuals within it.

Sociology/Family/978-0-375-71381-1

VINTAGE BOOKS
Available from your local bookstore, or visit
www.randomhouse.com